CATCH THE FIRE

Guy Chevreau has served the Baptist Church since 1979. He received his Th.D. from Wycliffe College, Toronto School of Theology, having studied in the area of the history of theology. He regularly teaches at the Toronto Airport Vineyard pastors' days, and now serves as teaching adjunct at the Airport Vineyard. He is married to Janis; they have two children, Graham and Caitlin. When it's windy enough, Guy is likely to be found out in Lake Ontario, windsurfing his brains out.

DEDICATION

The great composer, J.S. Bach began many of his compositions with the letters, *J.J.*, and ended with *S.D.G.* These were Latin abbreviations for 'Jesu Juva' and 'Soli Deo Gloria' – 'Jesus help me', and 'To God alone be the glory'.

In that same spirit of humility and gratitude, this work is dedicated.

Guy Chevreau

CATCH THE FIRE

The Toronto Blessing

An experience of renewal and revival

Preface by John Arnott, Senior Pastor of the Toronto Airport Vineyard

Marshall Pickering
An Imprint of HarperCollins*Publishers*

Marshall Pickering is an Imprint of
HarperCollins*Religious*
Part of HarperCollins*Publishers*
77–85 Fulham Palace Road, London W6 8JB

First published in Great Britain
in 1994 by Marshall Pickering

1 3 5 7 9 10 8 6 4 2

Quotations are taken from the
Revised English Bible

A catalogue record for this book is
available from the British Library

ISBN 0 551 02923-4

Typeset by Harper Phototypesetters Limited,
Northampton, England
Printed and bound in Great Britain by
HarperCollinsManufacturing Glasgow

CONTENTS

PREFACE

No one is more surprised by this recent outpouring of the Holy Spirit than my wife Carol and I. We are utterly amazed at what God has done in and through our church these last seven months. Certainly it has gone far beyond anything we ever envisioned or imagined those first few weeks! Every night, as we look over the crowd, we are awed at the number of people who have come, so very hungry for what God has for them. Over the course of their stay with us, most of them are impacted in some way or another, many with life-transforming impartations of the Holy Spirit, from which they will never recover. Again and again, we hear powerful testimonies to the radically transforming grace of God. To Him be all the glory!

Whether it is rededications, or first-time conversations, remarkable physical healings or deep emotional restoration, the people are much more deeply in love with Jesus, and find a renewed hunger for the Word and for prayer.

Administratively, what we are seeing is a nameless and faceless moving of the Spirit. It doesn't matter who is preaching. Many different speakers have led the meetings, and the outcome is always the same. After worship, testimonial interviews, and the preaching of the Word of God, the Holy Spirit comes and powerfully touches and transforms lives. It is not a consequence of great or prominent personalities.

And while the physical manifestations that have accompanied the Spirit's outpouring in our midst are abundant and varied, we have endeavoured to shift the focus off them, and appreciate rather the inward work of grace and empowering that is always the result.

We are thrilled with the worldwide impact of this move of the Spirit: thousands of pastors and leaders have come from so many different countries around the world and have been touched by the power of the Spirit. Upon returning home, they have not only discovered that their own lives are transformed, but also that of their churches, as the Holy Spirit has come and been poured out upon them afresh. Our constant prayer is that this time of refreshing will increase both in depth and in breadth until the earth will be filled with the knowledge of the glory of the Lord as the waters cover the sea (Habakkuk 2:14). This has already started – it is so life-giving that denominational differences have melted into obscurity, as a fresh love for Jesus has become pre-eminent; leaders of every denominational persuasion have come and drunk deeply of this fresh outpouring. The Holy Spirit is the only true unifier!

Our own staff and ministry team have of course made all of the protracted meetings possible, often working into the wee hours of the morning, 'giving it away'. Many have been the letters and cards saying *'Special thanks to the ministry team'*; they have gone the extra mile again and again. Without their faithful service, we could never have continued. Many other local churches, Vineyards and otherwise, have also helped out in numerous ways, loaning us their staff members and their worship teams so that we have enjoyed good organization, ministry teams and worship every night. Special thanks also go to Randy Clark, his family, and the St Louis Vineyard for allowing him to stay in Toronto for prolonged periods of time during the first two months, enabling us to get the fire really burning.

We are deeply grateful to Guy Chevreau whom we have come to know as a good and faithful friend, as well as a very able scholar. Until just recently, Guy was pastoring a Baptist church plant in Oakville, Ontario. He has a ThD in historical theology, and has studied the renewing work of the Spirit of God for many years, yet had never been part of a revival. Since the attendance at his first meeting in early February 1994, he has become part of the Renewal team; we are especially grateful for Guy's teaching on Jonathan Edwards at the Wednesday pastors' and leaders' afternoon. He is well able to assemble the various threads and components of the Airport Vineyard story and the various acts of the Holy Spirit as He has worked among us. Guy has put this together in a beautiful volume that we believe will be informative and helpful, both in understanding the early beginnings of this present outpouring as well as providing helpful and resourceful insights to all who would desire more understanding of the deeper things of God.

Carol and I are grateful beyond words; the Holy Spirit has proved His faithfulness again and again and again. Our prayer is that He will not only continue to move among us, but will also begin to move powerfully in *your* life. As you seek for more of Him, may this book impart to you a fresh revelation of His wondrous works, and renewed hope that *you too* may enter in and do the works of Jesus in the power of the Spirit. May His kingdom come and His will be done *on earth* as it is in heaven.

All Glory to Jesus Christ, the Son of God, our Risen Saviour and Lord.

John Arnott
Senior Pastor
Toronto Airport Vineyard
28 August 1994

ACKNOWLEDGEMENTS

By God's grace, it has been my privilege to spend much of the summer researching, reading and writing. For me, it was exactly what I needed. My children, Graham and Caitlin, however, got a little less Dad than they expected over the holidays, but we had a longer time together. Thanks go to them for their understanding, and for the fun we had as we played at our many games.

Thanks to my wife Janis, too. For the practical help in copy typing and proofreading, and the much larger revisioning of expectations, and the scramble to go with the flow – I bless you.

Though I know they don't want it, I would be remiss if I didn't acknowledge my gratitude to 'B' and 'L' for their belief in me, and their very practical help on the front end of things.

To Jeremy Sinnott, Ian Ross, Gary Patton, Judy Greenough and Dr Chris Page, thank you for your ruthlessness with my syntax; I take full responsibility for any and all counsel unheeded!

Beyond the writing of the book, my debt of gratitude extends to Randy Clark, for his faithfulness to the Lord's call on his life, his openness and vulnerability, his friendship and counsel, and his willingness to let me play 'Elisha' and tag along behind and learn; to the staff at Airport Vineyard, for their love and acceptance, their generosity, their infinite grace under pressure, and their zeal for the Spirit of revival; and to the ministry team, for their open-hearted love and inter-cessions.

Lastly, the acceptance, care, honour and encouragement I have received from John and Carol Arnott leaves me thanking God for them every time they come to mind.

Guy Chevreau
29 August 1994

CHAPTER ONE

DRAWN OUT

A Prologue

Now unto Him who is able to do immeasurably more than all we can ask or conceive, by the power which is at work among us, to Him be glory in the church and in Christ Jesus from generation to generation evermore! Amen. (Ephesians 3:20-21)

We all have our favourite authors; Annie Dillard is one of mine. She's a favourite because her reflections and musings strike deep to the heart of life and living; she 'sees' and 'feels' with an aliveness that calls life up and out of me. In her book *Teaching a Stone to Talk,* Dillard reflects on her worship experiences at church: 'It is the second Sunday in Advent . . . No one, least of all the organist, could find the opening hymn. Then no one knew it. Then no one could sing it anyways . . . There was no sermon, only announcements.' (p. 37).

With almost unguarded abandon, she wonders about the incredible contrast, even the danger, of assembling and praying, for instance, the Sanctus:

Holy, Holy, Holy Lord,
God of power and might,
heaven and earth are full of your glory . . .

> Why do we people in churches seem like cheerful, brainless tourists on a packaged tour of the Absolute? . . . On the whole, I do not find Christians, outside of the catacombs, sufficiently sensible of conditions. Does anyone have the foggiest idea what sort of power we so blithely invoke? Or, as I suspect, does no one believe a word of it? The churches are children playing on the floor with their chemistry sets, mixing up a batch of TNT to kill a Sunday morning. It is madness to wear ladies' straw hats and velvet hats to church; we should all be wearing crash helmets. Ushers should issue life preservers and signal flares; they should lash us to our pews. For the sleeping god (sic) may wake someday and take offence, or the waking god (sic) may draw us out to where we can never return.

This book is all about being 'drawn out to where we can never return'.[1]

And just so you know, *Catch the Fire* is not an objective documentation of a remarkable move of God, with theological and historical perspectives brought to bear; I write first and foremost as one who has been 'drawn out to where *I* can never return'.

[1] *Teaching a Stone to Talk*, p. 58.

I became a Christian in 1972, through the non-denominational high school ministry to unchurched kids, 'Young Life'. I started going because there were lots of pretty girls; I stayed for the relational care I received. After several months, I asked one of the leaders what it was that he had that I didn't; he answered, 'Christ,' and shared the Gospel with me. Several months after that, in a particularly unhappy frame of mind, I said, 'God, if You're there, I've made a mess of things. You can have my life if You want it, and do with it what You want.'

Not a particularly orthodox confession of faith, but it was a beginning. I started reading the New Testament, and one of the questions I had for my new friends who were discipling me was, 'Does Jesus still heal people today?' I was told basically that 'miracles finished with the death of the first apostles, that they weren't needed now. We had the preaching of the Word to build faith.' It took me eighteen years to get that one sorted out.

In my early twenties, I was wondering what to do with my life vocationally. I read philosophy as an undergraduate, and Saturday mornings, my father would mumble from behind the job listings in *The Globe and Mail,* 'No jobs for Philosopher Kings this week.'

In my devotions, I was reading through the Old Testament. When I came to Ezra 7:10, it was as if the Spirit of God mugged me: *'Ezra set his heart to study the Law, to practise it, and to teach statute and ordinance to Israel.' That's* what I wanted to do with my life. The following fall, I was off to seminary.

I'm grateful for my years at divinity college, and forever

indebted to three of my professors for all that they imparted. But some of the curriculum has proven problematic. For instance, two of the courses we had to take were Homiletics I and II, 'How to Preach', and, 'Practice Preaching'. The second of these was brutal: two class hours every Thursday afternoon, and in those two hours, four sermons would be delivered and critiqued, back to back. You knew that if you were the last guy up, you'd get carved to pieces, no matter how stellar your pulpiteering. The way we were taught to preach was essentially: introduction, three points and a poem. The issue was *persuasion.* One of our texts on preaching was: *Reaching People from the Pulpit.*

When I graduated from seminary in 1981, I went to McAdam, a small town in rural New Brunswick. I tried to be as persuasive a preacher as I could be, and I learned a great deal from the congregation at Rockland Drive. While there, the Spirit of God impressed on me another 'life text', this time from 1 Corinthians 4:20: *'The Kingdom of God is not a matter of talk but of power.'* This time, however, the passage was far more unsettling than it was inspiring. Truth to tell, it messed me up. As I examined my pulpit ministry, and all that I was about as a parish pastor, it left me crying out, 'God, there's got to be something more.'

The hunger was such that I went and completed a ThD. in Christian spirituality, thinking that a study of the 'masters' would open up some of that 'more'. Again, I'm both grateful and indebted for the opportunity to work at that depth and breadth. But . . . I didn't discover what I was seeking. That more. My *words* about the Kingdom just got a little smarter. I had access to greater background, and developed a larger perspective on things, but nothing more of the Apostle's 'Kingdom power'.

I next served First Baptist Church, Niagara Falls, and attempted to bring renewal and re-missioning to a hundred-year-old work. In terms of my preaching . . . once in a while, people would laugh. Once in a while, people would get teary-eyed. Once in a while, people would be persuaded. But I was growing more and more dissatisfied with my 'ministry' and its lack of influence.

During my time at Niagara, I was invited to a church growth seminar in Guelph. Mike Turrigiano, the 'feature preacher' was introduced, and in terms of first impressions, he carried himself as though he'd come in on a very long 'red-eye' flight, and looked like he was, perhaps permanently, wrinkled.

He quickly captivated my attention. In a thick Bronx accent, he proceeded to tell of inner-city ministry to heroin addicts, of sharing Jesus with them, and their lives getting turned around. Of 'loving on' prostitutes as they'd never been loved on; of praying for the sick, and seeing them healed; of deliverance ministry – something that seminary training had completely demythologized.

I was shaking my head the whole time.

I've never recovered.

And I'm forever in Mike's debt.

The Apostle Paul's testimony comes to mind every time I think of Mike:

> The word I spoke, the gospel I proclaimed, did not sway you with clever arguments; but with a demonstration of the Spirit's power, so that your faith might be built not on human wisdom but on the power of God . . . I speak God's hidden wisdom, His secret purpose framed from the very beginning to bring us to our destined glory . . . Scripture speaks of 'things beyond our seeing, things beyond our hearing, things beyond our understanding, all prepared by God for those who love Him; and these are what God has revealed to us through the Spirit . . . And we have received this Spirit from God . . . so that we may know all that God has lavished upon us . . .' (1 Corinthians 2:4–5, 7, 9–10, 12).

Mike was doing the stuff of the Kingdom of God, demonstrating the Gospel. I could only theologize about it, and that from a de-supernaturalized perspective. I had no expectation that 'signs and wonders' were for today's proclamation of the good news; I certainly had no experience of anything like a demonstration of the Gospel with power.

Mike talked some about someone named John Wimber. Until then, I'd never heard of him. But Mike had left such an impression on me that I ordered and read Wimber's books, *Power Evangelism* and *Power Healing,* and did extended historical research as corroboration and complement. I had done my doctoral dissertation on John Calvin's instruction on private prayer, and because of my familiarity with his writings, I started there. Calvin can be counted as one of the foremost architects of Protestant theology, and as such, he lays for us the theological foundations on which many of us build our faith. Foundations being what they are, most of us don't see them, or even realize they're there, buried as they are. But aware of them or not, they carry our expectations and frame our experience.

Two passages in Calvin's writings speak volumes as to our evangelical legacy. From his *Commentary* on Matthew 10:1-10, the passage where Jesus empowers His disciples for the proclamation and demonstration of the Gospel, and then sends them out, Calvin says that they were

> employed as assistants only, to secure attention to Him where His voice could not reach; afterwards, He will commit into their hands the office of *teaching* which He had discharged. It is of great importance to observe this, that we may not suppose it to be a certain and fixed rule laid down for all ministers of the word, when our Lord gives instructions to the preachers of His doctrine as to what He wishes them to do for a short time.[2]

Interpreting Calvin's comments, what he's saying is, *we* ought not to expect to be able to heal and deliver. What Calvin lays down is that miracles were a front-end dynamic only. Similar instruction is found in his life's

[2] John Calvin, *A Commentary on the Harmony of the Evangelists*, vol. II, the Calvin Translation Society, Baker Book House, Grand Rapids, Michigan, 1979, p.428.

work, *The Institutes of the Christian Religion.* The following passage is from his work on the sacraments, specifically his comments on the laying on of hands.

> Assuredly the Holy Spirit is still present among God's people, for the church cannot stand unless He is its guide and director . . .. But those miraculous powers and manifest workings, which were dispensed by the laying on of hands, have ceased. *They have rightly lasted only for a time.* For it was fitting that the new preaching of the gospel, and the new Kingdom of Christ should be illumined and magnified by unheard-of and extraordinary miracles. When the Lord ceased from these, He did not utterly forsake His church, but declared that the magnificence of His Kingdom and the dignity of His word had been excellently enough disclosed.[3]

Things become clearer still when one learns that in Calvin's mother-tongue, French, the common idiom 'to go to church' was 'aller au sermon'. Without question, teaching had centre-stage by way of expectation. And while Calvin characteristically draws strength from his work with the early Church Fathers, his reading of the cessation of healing ministry is certainly skewed. It just wasn't the case for the Church Fathers. Two samples suffice: around AD 250, one hundred and fifty years or so

[3] John Calvin, *The Institutes of the Christian Religion*, IV. 19.6; trans. F.L. Battles, The Library of Christian Classics, XXI, Westminster Press, Philadelphia, 1960, p.1454, emphasis added.

after the death of the last of the apostles, Novatian served the Roman presbytery. He wrote a work titled, *A Treatise Concerning the Trinity.* In the section on the Holy Spirit and spiritual gifts, chapter 29, he begins his instruction by citing the prophet Joel: 'In the last days, I will pour out my Spirit . . ..' Novatian writes of promise and fulfilment, and contrasts the two times before and after the Lord's resurrection:

> In the former, He [the Spirit] was occasional, in the latter, always. In the former not always being in them [the prophets and apostles], in the latter as abiding always in them; and in the former distributed with reserve, in the latter all poured out; in the former given sparingly, in the latter liberally bestowed; not yet manifested before the Lord's resurrection, but conferred after the Lord's resurrection.

He then works from the Farewell Discourses in John's Gospel, where Jesus promises 'the Advocate, the Spirit of Truth' (John 14:16–17; 15:20; 16:7, 13). Novatian writes:

> This is He who strengthened their hearts and minds . . . who was in them the enlightener of divine things . . . they were armed by the same Spirit, having in themselves the gifts which this same Spirit distributes, and appropriates to the Church. This is He [the Spirit] who places prophets in the Church, instructs teachers, directs tongues, gives powers and healings, does wonderful works, offers discrimination of spirits . . .

> and orders and arranges whatever other gifts there are of *charismata;* and thus makes the Lord's Church everywhere, and in all, perfect and completed.[4]

Note that the tense of the verbs in this passage changes from past tense, when he speaks of the early Church, to present tense, when he describes immediate expectation and experience. If we read between the lines, it seems that for Novatian, no Spirit – no supernatural gifts – no Church.

Augustine served as Bishop in North Africa from AD 393 to 430; geographically, his influence was felt over all of western Christendom. Historically, Augustine has charted the course of theological understanding of Christian faith more than any other theologian, second only to the Apostle Paul. His work profoundly influenced Luther and Calvin, to name only two other theological heavyweights. Augustine's work, *The City of God* has been described as 'the masterpiece of the greatest genius among the Latin Fathers.'[5] In it, he has a thirteen-page account of healings and deliverances he has personally witnessed. The section is titled: 'Of miracles which were wrought that the world might believe in Christ, miracles which have not ceased since the world believed.' He tells of the blind receiving their sight, healings of breast cancer, gout, kidney stones, and hernias; of the restoration of a

[4] Novatian, *A Treatise Concerning the Trinity,* ed. Alexander Roberts, *Ante-Nicene Fathers, vol.5,* Hendrickson Publishers, 1994, p.640.
[5] Philip Schaff, *Preface* to Augustine's *The City of God,* ed. Philip Schaff, *Nicene and Post-Nicene Fathers, vol.2,* Hendrickson Publishers, 1994, p.v.

little boy run over and crushed by an ox cart; and of the demonized delivered. He then writes:

> What am I to do? I am so pressed by the promise of finishing this work [his book, *The City of God*] that I cannot record all the miracles I know . . .

He then goes on for four more pages . . . and concludes:

> Even now, therefore, many miracles are wrought, the same God who wrought those we read of [in the gospels] still performing them, *by* whom He will, and *as* He will.'[6]

As all of this reading and research spilled over into my preaching, we saw some people physically restored. While working through a sermon series on the healing ministry of Jesus in Luke's Gospel, one of our senior members removed her infra-red hearing headset, and placed it on the pew beside her. She looked at her husband, grinning from ear to ear. Tears began streaming down his cheeks. Both of them looked up at me, their faces beaming. While proclaiming the healing ministry of Jesus, the Lord had sovereignly healed her of her deafness, restoring 80 per cent of her hearing. And while we saw other less dramatic, but no less significant, healings, we were also thrown into the arena of spiritual warfare. Suffice it to say that the learning curve went straight up.

[6] *Ibid.*, XXII.8, pp. 484-491.

Along with Wimber's books, I was reading other church growth material: on leadership, innovation, infrastructure, time management, goal setting and strategic planning, paradigm shifts and mission philosophy. There were some very helpful, absolutely necessary things learned. Several years later, I resigned from a traditional, parish-based ministry and moved to a church plant setting, where it was hoped that we would have greater freedom to grow a church that was unapologetic in its purpose: to be a supernaturally gifted and missioned community of faith, gathered to reach the unchurched through intentional relational evangelism. Lamentably, we faced a 'crisis of wineskins'. Personally, the winter of '94 was one of the most demanding periods of my life, and left me feeling like I'd been 'ridden hard and put away wet'. By early May, it was obvious that the work would not be viable, and we terminated the mission the following month.

The last weekend of January '94, my wife Janis went to a women's retreat. There, she heard reports of an 'unusual' move of the Spirit at the Toronto Airport Vineyard. I had been to the Airport a few times on other, previous occasions; I knew some of the people there, and respected and honoured what I had seen of the leadership. As Janis relayed the experiences of some folks that we knew, things sounded VERY FLAKY. What was being described was that people were coming under an anointing so powerful that it left them 'drunk in the Spirit'. They were falling about, laughing hysterically.

The next night, we came to the Airport meeting. I

came, more desperate than curious, and too desperate to be critical. As a Baptist pastor, I personally had not seen anything much by way of a physical manifestation of the Spirit's power or presence, other than some quiet tears once in a while. It is an understatement to say that I was personally unfamiliar with the kinds of physical manifestations we saw at the Airport meetings – uncontrollable laughter and inconsolable weeping; violent shaking and falling down; people waving their arms around, in windmill-like motions, or vigorous judo-like chopping with their forearms.

As we kept coming back, the question I was forced to answer was what I expected, what would it be like, for the Spirit of God to bring personal and corporate renewal? I knew it wasn't a sermon from a master preacher; nor would it come from another conference, or from that missing set of lecture notes. I'd been around those blocks before. Having concluded that it would be something different, I could not bring closure to what I was touching at the meetings.

That, and the fact that Janis 'took the joy'. That's not exactly the whole story. She was down on the floor, repeatedly, hysterical with laughter. At one point, John Arnott, the senior pastor at the Airport Vineyard, prayed that she would stay in this state for forty-eight hours. She was that, and more – at times unable to walk a straight line, certainly unfit to drive, or to host the guests that came for dinner the next evening.

Typically, she is able to prepare the meal ahead of time so that we can focus our energies on those visiting. When

I returned home from work that particular night, the kitchen looked very unready for dinner – there was no food in sight, and when I asked after the meal, Janis nearly fell to the floor in hysterical laughter. I went out to buy fish and chips.

On my return, our guests were already seated at the table. Without any place settings, Janis proceeded to toss hot, greasy fish to each of us; she dumped the box of french fries in the middle of the table, and then pushed little piles in our respective directions, all the while, finding *everything* VERY funny.

The next evening, I came forward for prayer – an invitation had been issued for anyone in pastoral ministry. I 'went down', yielding to the feelings of weakness and heaviness. With no cognitive or emotive content, I lay there thinking, 'I don't know . . . the guy that prayed for me had a pretty heavy hand . . . did I get pushed?' When I came forward for prayer the second time, I was in a bad mood. Again I went down, and as I lay there, I said, 'God, I don't care if this is You or not . . . I am so tired, I'm just going to lie here a while.'

The third time was at the mid-week pastors' meeting. Randy Clark, the guest preacher, had done some teaching, had answered some questions, and then offered to pray for us. We lined up at the front of the church.

He simply came up to Janis, and she was down on the floor, loony tunes, again. Randy prayed very gently, very quietly for me, and I went over, feeling too tired to stand any longer. As I lay there, I started weeping. Wailing, if the truth be told, for something like forty minutes. While there were no conscious, cognitive pictures, or images, memories or impressions, a long-standing bitterness and resentment was lifted in the process. That, and a sense that I had been released a little further into a new sense of God's sovereign authority and providential care over my life.

While many Pentecostals would say that I had been 'slain in the Spirit', the expression they commonly use to describe the experience of falling down under the power of the Spirit, Francis McNutt's term 'resting in the Spirit' seemed to fit my experience better. The depth of peace that was experienced brought life, not death; 'resting in the Spirit', however, doesn't serve to describe the empowerment I experienced as my body shook uncontrollably while lying there.

Later that afternoon, I 'heard' in my spirit a 'spoken' recommission from the Lord, clearer than I've ever heard the Lord speak before. Half an hour later, two men with prophetic ministries, Larry Randolf and Marc Dupont, spoke for a while, and then offered to bring their ministries to bear. Janis and I were the first two that they called up to the front of the sanctuary. The only way to describe the experience is that Larry read from my journal for the last three years, and Marc spoke the stuff of which I'll be writing during the next three years. As never before, we were, in the words of 1 Corinthians 14:3, 'built up, stimulated and encouraged'. Given what the next few months came to hold, we would have been in deep weeds without the sustaining hope that was imparted that afternoon.

On average, we have attended meetings two evenings a week, as well as the Wednesday pastors' afternoons. I regularly receive prayer; typically, there is little by way of physical manifestation. Much of the time, I remain standing while someone on the ministry team prays for me. Sunday 8 May was an exception. Pastors were again called forward for prayer; this time, I fell forward. As I lay on my face, someone stood over me, praying in the Spirit. Something wet fell on my cheek; I thought that in their exuberance, that *something* had flown out of their mouth and landed on me. Then, with the command of the revelatory, I realized that it wasn't what I thought it was, but, rather, a tear. I began to weep, and did so for the next three-and-a-half hours. I am forever in debt to Carol Arnott for the care I received from her that night – she sat on the floor at my side throughout the evening, interceding, ministering, and *releasing* more than I'll ever know. What I am aware of was that I received a fuller revelation of my Heavenly Father's love, lavished upon me in Christ, and with that, a settling of some issues of control and self-determination. What I 'felt' that night was that something of Ezekiel's 'new heart' had been imparted to me (Ezekiel 36:26–27), by times with physical chest pains that were so intense, I could not help but cry aloud.

Since our first meeting at the Airport Vineyard in February, there is no question in my mind that God has worked some deep restoration within me, such that 'old things HAVE passed away; new things have come' (1 Corinthians 5:17); the new sense of intimacy with Jesus is precious beyond words, and a renewed hunger for the Word is itself reviving; there has come a new hope and confidence in my Father's sovereign authority and providential care over my life and ministry; a sense of His favour and pleasure in me as His son; and with all of that, I now have at least something of an experiential grid for the Spirit's ministry in our midst, doing not just MORE, but 'immeasurably more than all we can ask or conceive . . .' (Ephesians 3:20). And as I reflect on things, I keep coming to the Airport meetings because there's a gap. A gap between the way the Apostle Paul brought the Gospel, and my experience of ministry. Or, more accurately, my non-experience. But like Dillard says, 'I've been drawn out to where I can never return.'

This book, aside from this prologue, is not MY story. Thousands have been drawn out, to where they can never return. Since the first of the meetings with Randy Clark on 20 January, 1994, the Airport Vineyard has been host to a renewing move of God that has brought a long-awaited revival of faith, hope and love. There has been a most notable release of freedom and healing, joy and power – protracted meetings have been held every night but Mondays. As of 1st September 1994, intentionally conservative estimates count a cumulative attendance total of 90,000; 30,000 are first-time attenders. Over 400 local pastors have come, at least to investigate; over 4,000 pastors, spouses and leaders from all over continental North America, and as far away as Britain, Chile,

Argentina, Switzerland, France, Germany, Scandinavia, South Africa, Nigeria, Kenya, Japan, New Zealand and Australia have come to receive the outpouring . . . and while virtually impossible to track, the ministry teams have made contact with at least 2,000 'prodigals' who have come forward for prayer as they re-commit their lives; over 450 have made first-time professions of faith.

These statistics are calculated on the following basis: nearly every night, the congregation is asked the following questions: 'How many of you are here for the first time?' 'Where are some of you from?' 'How many of you are pastors, spouses and leaders?' Similar questions are asked at the Wednesday afternoon pastors' and leaders' meetings, and opportunity is given to those in attendance to submit names and addresses for a mailing list. Cumulative attendance is calculated by multiplying the sanctuary seating – 400, by the number of days, 225; this is only an average, given that it neither accounts for the fifteen meetings for which larger facilities have been rented, nor for the last two months where there has been standing room only for over a hundred people. These are easy numbers to produce; more problematic logistically is the tracking of 'prodigals' and first-time conversations. A specially trained ministry team makes every attempt to meet, counsel, pray for and follow up those who come forward for ministry. There is no way of knowing the numbers who have made private commitments and rededications.

In the wake of a defeated, discouraged and characteristically exhausted Christian experience, thousands of believers have returned to their 'first love' (Revelation 2:4). Many have experienced, with this restored intimacy with the Lord, a renewing of commit-ment and call, an enlarging and clarification of spiritual vision, and a rekindled passion for Jesus and the work of the Kingdom. Thousands of desperate and burned-out pastors and their spouses have received a refreshing, a re-commissioning, and an anointing . . . hence the title of the book, *Catch the Fire.*

Some of the physical manifestations accompanying this move of God are unsettling, leaving many feeling that they have no grid for evaluation, no map to guide. After a short introduction to the Airport Vineyard, what follows is a three-part piece: in the first section, a biblical foundation for renewal and revival is laid; the second sets an historical context, drawing from the writings of Jonathan Edwards, the theological architect of the Great Awakening. The final section is a chronicling of some local personal testimonies, as well as a documentation of the impact this impartation has had on congregations as visiting pastors and leaders return home, and the dynamisms are 'catalytically transferred'. The concluding chapter serves as summary and synthesis.

It is my prayer that as you read what follows, your heart is stirred to want MORE.

CHAPTER TWO

GETTING TO KEEP WHAT THEY GIVE AWAY

A Short Introduction to the Toronto Airport Vineyard

> *Would any father among you offer his son a snake when he asks for a fish, or a scorpion when he asks for an egg? If you . . . know how to give good things to your children, how much more will the heavenly father give the Holy Spirit to those who ask Him!* (Luke 11:11–13)

One of the questions that's repeatedly asked is, 'Why would God choose the Toronto Airport Vineyard for this outpouring?' John Arnott, the founder and senior pastor of the church, grins sheepishly, and answers, 'I wish I could tell you that it's a consequence of our intercessory prayers. We wish we could say that we've had an active part in ushering in this move of God, but it hasn't been the case. It has been God's sovereign choosing.'

I have the highest regard for John and his wife Carol; they are some of the most gracious, generous and humble people I know. They have remarkably open hearts to the whole Body of Christ, and have incredible hunger for the Spirit of God. Their greatest desire has been to see the Body of Christ come into a vital outpouring of the Holy

Spirit, and they have sought to learn and receive from those who are able to demonstrate the presence and power of God in their ministries, and have themselves worked diligently to that end.

Back in the late '60s and early '70s, John was significantly impacted by Kathryn Kuhlman's ministry, and later on, Benny Hinn's, which began in Toronto. While there was much to process, he was deeply impressed with the fruit, the results of these ministries, for he saw hundreds of people receive a powerful, life-transforming touch from the Lord. He went to many of their meetings, and in significant ways they laid an imprint for the future direction and conduct of his ministry.

In 1980, John and Carol went to Indonesia on a ministry trip, and had such an engaging time, they felt like they wanted to move their vocational commitments from business to the work of ministry. Soon after their return, they were called to plant an independent church, in Stratford, Ontario, Carol's home town. It was loosely structured on a Calvary Chapel model, and, with the Lord's blessing, it was not long before they were serving full time. In 1986, they went to a John Wimber Conference in Vancouver, and another in Ohio, and immediately began relating with the Vineyard, officially joining them in early 1987. Several aspects of Wimber's ministry drew them: his personal honesty and transparency, his humility and approachability, and most of all, his commitment to empowering every believer for Kingdom ministry. At that point, John believed that 'even he' could move in the supernatural things of the Spirit.

That same year, they began a kinship house group in west Toronto, John's home town. They were joined by Jeremy and Connie Sinnott, who, with their gifts in worship teamed well with the Arnotts. The Toronto church grew while the Arnotts commuted between the two plants in Stratford and Toronto. By the summer of '92, the Toronto work had grown such that both John and Jeremy could serve full time; leadership in Stratford was in place, and John turned that work over to Jerry Steingard, one of the associate pastors there. Both churches prospered, and the Arnotts concentrated on raising up, training and equipping both a staff and a ministry team.

The Airport Vineyard has been through the inner healing and deliverance learning curve, and in many ways the church has seen its growth through the conferences it has hosted; the intention, however, has not only been to gather and build up the local Body for ministry, but to be an encouragement to as much of the larger Body of Christ as possible.

In September of 1992, Carol and John went to several of Benny Hinn's meetings in Toronto. John had become friends with Benny years ago, at the outset of his ministry in Toronto. Longing for a similar kind of empowerment that would enable them to demonstrate God's Kingdom authority in people's lives, they joined the crowd at Maple Leaf Gardens. The Arnotts watched with awe as 1,000 or more gave their lives to Christ, and they left the meeting with the conviction that, 'Yes, we do have a mighty God. He is able to reach the city of Toronto. He can do it in power and might.'

Later the following year, June of 1993, they were in Texas visiting John's daughters, and went to a Rodney Howard Browne meeting. Rodney is a South African Pentecostal evangelist whose ministry has been characterized by the outbreak of 'holy laughter'. At the meeting in Fort Worth, a call was issued to all of the pastors and their spouses. About 200 came forward. Rodney moved down the line, praying, 'Fill. Fill. Fill', and when all the smoke cleared there was John and one other man still standing. That had become typical – be it at the Hinn meetings, or other ministry opportunities – while others were 'falling under the power', John would be left standing. Repeatedly, he would wonder, 'Lord, what's the issue of my heart?'

A significant breakthrough came in November of 1993, when John, Carol and a ministry team went to Argentina. There they met Claudio Freidzon, the head of the Pentecostal Assemblies of God in Argentina. He had gone to a Benny Hinn meeting and came home powerfully anointed, something that John had been longing to do. Claudio was ministering to the Hispanics in Argentina, but at a conference the Arnotts attended, he prayed for all of the visitors first. John and Carol went up, and as John puts it, 'Carol went flying'.

He himself fell down, but instantly began to analyze things: 'Lord, was this really You, or did I just go with it because I want You so badly? What am I supposed to do? I don't know if I am supposed to stand, fall, roll or forget it?'

After John got up off the floor, Claudio came over to

him. John was standing with his hands up, posturing his openness to the Lord, and Claudio looked at him and said, 'Do you want it?' He said, 'Yes. I really want it.' Then Claudio said, 'Then take it!' and he slapped John on both of his hands. John fell again. But this time he dialed down a lot of the analysis and said, 'I don't care, I'm just going to take what God has to give.' Something clicked in his heart at that moment. It was as though he heard the Lord say, 'For goodness sake, will you take it? It's yours.' John realized then that there is a faith component that has a part to play; simply desiring the Spirit's outpouring is not enough. Empowered with the Spirit's anointing, one must step into a certain arena of ministry.

That same month, at the annual meeting of the association of Vineyard churches, one of the regional overseers, Happy Leman, shared the results of October's regional meeting with John Arnott; they had experienced a powerful demonstration of God's presence at the meeting. The initiator of the outbreak, humanly speaking, was Randy Clark, the founding pastor of the Vineyard Christian Fellowship in St Louis, Missouri. After years of seeing little fruit and power in his ministry, Randy had become desperately hungry for God. Hearing of unusual manifestations of God's presence through Rodney Howard Browne's ministry, Randy attended one of Rodney's meetings in Tulsa, Oklahoma. Randy was persistent in his pursuit of the Lord's renewing graces, and lined up repeatedly to receive prayer. Five months later, at a Browne meeting Randy attended in Lakeland, Forida, Rodney discerned a powerful anointing being released in

Randy's life – he came over to him and said, 'This is the fire of God in your hands; go home and pray for everyone in your church.' The first Sunday of Randy's return, he did as instructed, and saw a similar outbreak of the Spirit as he ministered. At the regional meeting of the mid-western Vineyard churches, Happy Leman asked Randy to share what was happening in his church, and when they turned the meeting to a ministry time, many of those gathered experienced a beautiful release of joy and power. John immediately asked Randy to come to Toronto to speak and join with him to minister in January.

The day before Randy left for Toronto, he received a call from a friend, Richard Holcomb. Richard had played a significant role in Randy's life over the last ten years, repeatedly bringing timely encouragement. Richard had no idea of what was taking place in Randy's life at the time, but felt that the Lord had a word for Randy: 'Test Me now, test Me now, test Me now. Do not be afraid; I will back you up. I want your eyes to be opened to My resources in the heavens just as Elisha asked for Gehazi's eyes to be opened. And do not be anxious, because when you become anxious you cannot hear Me.' It is an understatement to say that Randy's faith was built up by that word.

John's initial invitation was for four days; that extended to ten. Randy was greatly used of God to ignite the renewal, and served, on and off, through February till mid-March, until it was imperative that he return to his family and home church in St Louis.

While it was initially feared that the renewal

dynamisms were dependent on Randy's presence, a remarkable transferability was soon discovered. Mid-February, John and Carol were booked to lead an out-of-town healing conference, and when they began sharing what was taking place at home, people started laughing, and it wasn't long before similar refreshing was experienced. When overseas in Hungary at the end of that month, the Arnotts saw renewal break out there. As pastors and leaders began to come to the Airport for a time of refreshing, many would send back reports that on their return home, the Spirit was manifesting similar dynamics of renewal and revival. This book is subtitled *The Toronto Blessing*; that is the affectionate name that many British pastors and leaders have given to the impartation that has made such an impact on churches throughout Britain, beginning, many would say, with London's Holy Trinity Brompton, and the SouthWest London Vineyard.[1] Several accounts of the Spirit's renewing, reviving work are detailed in Chapter 5.

Guest preachers following Randy have included Larry Randolph, and Vineyard pastors, Mike Turrigiano, Happy Leman, Wes Campbell, Ralph Kucera and Ron Allen. They came not only to serve; they each testify having received great blessing and impartation, and have returned to their respective fellowships, and have been used as renewal 'fire-lighters' in their areas. John White and John Wimber have also been to the Airport Vineyard meetings, and have brought their experience, wisdom and

[1] See *The Church of England Newspaper*, June 17th, 1994; The main front page news story was headed 'Revival breaks out in London Churches'.

counsel to bear on the ourpouring.

Though both John and Randy came under Rodney Howard Browne's ministry, the conduct or model for the Airport meetings is significantly different, in that at Rodney's meetings, he is the only one praying for people. At the Airport, a team of thirty trained men and women pray for those who come forward to receive ministry. Because of a multiple team, more people can receive prayer more frequently at the Airport Vineyard; in fact, people are encouraged to come and receive, repeatedly; if they rest in the Spirit, they are encouraged to stay where they are on the floor, and 'soak' as members of the ministry team often return, and intercede again and again.

The various physical and emotional manifestations that literally thousands upon thousands have experienced – uncontrollable laughter, 'drunkenness' in the Spirit, intense weeping, falling to the floor, physical convulsions or 'jerks', pogoing and bouncing, shouting and roaring, visions, prophetic words and announcements, often accompanied with physical demonstrations – these manifestations are what immediately draw the first-time visitor's attention. There are always some who come, take a look, and conclude that the noise and the exuberance they witness are more fitting at a football game than a worship service; they shake their heads, and leave, mumbling in essence, 'I don't believe that's God, and I don't want it.'

But there are thousands and thousands who have come, and stayed long enough to enter into the worship process and evaluate the testimonies, attend to the preaching of the Word, and then respond to the invitation to receive prayer. The devotion and faith expectancy that pervades night after night is a beautiful thing to witness, and whether or not one 'likes' the manifestations that characterize the meetings, those testifying continue to declare that the Lord has met them personally with life-transforming consequences. Often, this is signalled by the manifestations, but they are only that – signals. It is as though an unfamiliar, non-verbal language is being used to describe and declare what the Spirit of God is doing in people's lives, whether it be refreshing and restoration, or healing, or a radical deepening of faith and hope, or recommission for ministry, or a power release for new aspects of ministry.

Concurrent with the Arnotts' experiences through 1992 and 1993, there were several prophetic pronouncements that anticipated this remarkable move of the Spirit that has been witnessed at the Airport Vineyard. Marc Dupont joined the staff of the Airport in the spring of 1992; his ministry is one of prophetic encouragement and instruction, both locally and internationally. The following is an edited transcription of his two-part prophecy, dated May 1992 and July 1993.

Part One: May '92, while in Toronto, for the area of Southern Ontario.

I. A vision of water falling over and on to an extremely large rock. The amount of the water was similar to Niagara Falls.

A. Toronto shall be a place where much living water will be flowing, even though at the present time both the church and the city are like big rocks – cold and hard, [and resistant] to God's love and His Spirit. The waterfall shall be so powerful that it will break the big rocks up into small stones that can be used in building the Kingdom. Those stones which resist the Spirit will be broken down into dust.

There will not be any true unity among the churches until they begin to respond to the prophetic call of the Father. The breaking of pride and stiffness will result in Christians and churches which can fit together [like stones] in the Master Builder's hands. At this moment, the 'living stones' are unable to fit together compactly because of major protrusions on the stones, which in effect keep the leaders at arm's length from one another. These protrusions are pride and arrogance.

[However,] church unity is going to be a growing and powerful vehicle for carrying forward the love of Christ to the city. There is going to be a new standard of co-operation among different pastors [as they do] outreach together and prayer together.

B. The rock in the vision shall be transformed from a rock of death into the rock of Psalm 40, and the rock that Jesus said would prevail against the gates of hell. As the people of God in Toronto cry out for God, the Lord is going to respond by placing their feet on His rock, [with a renewed sense] of intimacy with Him.

Our feet shall then be transformed into feet which can go forward with the Gospel against the gates of hell. Many will hear the new song that God will be putting in the mouths of His people and many will come to fear the Lord. A new song will spring up from the heart of the Church as we respond to the moving of the Holy Spirit. This is not so much a 'new song' literally, but a new freedom for worshipping with God's favour and presence resting on us. In that freedom, many churches will begin to take worship out into the public arenas, where the unchurched can hear. The artists and musicians of Toronto are going to experience a strong move of God's Spirit.

C. As in the time of Elijah, many who are privately going to the 'mountain' and seeking the face of the Lord are going to find that there are numerous others who are also deeply crying out to the Lord. Most of those who are really interceding and crying out to God are not 'mainstream'. Most of them are currently outside of the visible picture of what is happening right now. In late '93 and throughout '94, many ordinary Christians will, on their own, begin to form prayer groups to intercede for the city, the nation, and the peoples.

D. [Just as] the disciples of Jesus were gathered from many different areas of life, so the leaders of the coming move of the Lord are also going to be coming from many different areas. Many of them are also not mainstream, and many will be without a lot of previous experience, but they will end up both being used by God in evangelism, signs, and wonders, and also in discipling new converts.

[A great number of] traditional denominational pastors and churches are going to be in the forefront of the move of the Spirit that will take place. I believe that many Evangelical Pastors are going to have a tremendous prophetic anointing on their ministries and become the Lord's spokesmen to other pastors.

Many current leaders will not be the leaders of the coming move, because many of them will disqualify themselves by not responding to what the Father will be saying. As Jesus said, 'to those who have, more shall be given, and to those who do not have, even what they have will be taken away'!

E. Like Jerusalem, Toronto will be a centre from which many are sent out to the nations, on all continents. The Lord is going to be sending [out] many people, filled with His Spirit, [who are able to] demonstrate strong giftings, vision, and love. In the move that is coming, there are going to be new Bible schools, training centres, and leadership schools raised up. These schools will have a focus not only on Bible knowledge, but also in ministries of healing the broken hearts, and setting the captives free, and on developing intimacy with the Father.

II. As God's rock began to be raised up out of the stony city it began to be shaped like a huge dam, which stored the living water. At the same time, the water began to be poured out of the dam and began to flow west quite strongly.

I saw those waters like a strong raging river head west all the way to the Rocky Mountains, and then go north along the eastern edge of the mountains, and then go east again across the plains. In essence there was a huge circle of water that wrapped around the plains of Canada. As the waters originating from Toronto began to go into the plains areas, they began to find wells, or pockets of water in many areas of the plains. I believe these wells are symbolic of remnant areas of Mennonites and other groups that experienced revival years and years ago, but like deep unused wells have not been tapped for a long time. As these waters began to mix, the wells came to life and began to flow to many areas of the plains, and these areas became centres of revival which then spread to other cities and towns. I believe that there is a strong contingent of prayer warriors, who are descendants of people many years ago who sought the face of God for their country.

PART TWO: Update 5 July, 1993, while in Vancouver, Canada. More specifics for the present leadership of the Body of Christ in Toronto.

III. I believe the Lord indicated that the increase in evangelism, the moving of the Holy Spirit, and the call to intercessory prayer is going to happen even this summer and autumn, with the pace accelerating into the new year. At the same time, the refiner's fire is going to increase, [particularly] with current leadership. As [the question is asked] in Malachi 3, 'who can stand when the refiner's fire comes?', many leaders are going to be greatly shaken; they will basically go in two directions: one, more into a mode of prayer, waiting and listening to the Father, and acting out of obedience; or two, many will fall into temptation and sin, and will leave the ministry or bring judgement on themselves and their churches, which in turn will be greatly shaken, many to the point of falling apart. For those that begin to catch what the Spirit is saying to them, they are going to be taking radical steps that are going to be extremely [difficult] for those in the churches who are not hearing what the Spirit is saying.

I also sensed from the Lord an extreme danger for leaders who continue to [resist] the Holy Spirit. I believe that it is vital for Church leadership to be in humble prayer, for other leaders throughout Toronto.

IV. There are going to be two basic stages in this process, which are represented by the two stages in Ezekiel's vision of the valley of dry bones.

A. In the first stage, the dry bones will receive muscle, sinew and flesh. This is the prophetic stage, where the Church and the leaders begin to seek the Father and cry out to Him for grace, mercy and a sovereign move of His Spirit. It is during this time that leaders are going to come together for prayer, with a new attitude of humility as they realize that the Lord is calling us to do things which are completely beyond our abilities and past experiences. It is important to realize that when the Lord asked Ezekiel if the dry bones could come back to life, [he was unsure]; he merely responded that the Lord knew. In the same way the Father is going to be speaking things to leaders that will appear [equally as impossible] in our understanding of what can happen in our time and culture.

B. The second stage is the apostolic stage of power and authority coming on the Church in the Toronto area. There is going to be a move of the Spirit of God on the city that is going to include powerful signs and wonders, such as in the early days of the Church in Jerusalem. There are also going to be leaders raised up in the Body of Christ that are going to move in an authority that will be trans-denominational. They will be pastors of pastors, and will be recognized as spokesmen and leaders for the government of God in the Body of Christ across [all] denominational lines. It will only be when all of the five-fold offices of Ephesians [4:11] are in operation, and when church leaders are coming into unity in the Spirit, that there will be a powerful release of the Gospel through the Church to touch the cultures of Southern Ontario.

I believe that there is going to be a very strong freedom [to move in] miracles, healings, and signs and wonders, happening very consistently in the Body of Christ, and touching especially [the lives of] non-believers.

Though not as detailed, there were other prophetic declarations. One of the ministry team at the church Randy Clark pastors in St Louis was interceding for the meetings a week before Randy's arrival in Toronto. While in prayer, she had a vision of a map of North America which, as in the old TV show, *Ponderosa,* started on fire. The 'hot spot' was Toronto; the flames burnt a hole through the map there, and spread throughout Southern Ontario, and from there in all directions.

The question that opened this chapter was, 'Why would God choose the Airport Vineyard for this outpouring?' The short history outlined, and the description of the implicit values and priorities of the Airport's ministry, begin to address the question. To that is added the fact that everything rises or falls on leadership; John and Carol Arnott know what it is to be broken. They know, personally, the crying need for unconditional acceptance. They have beautiful, humble spirits, and are well aware of their continual need to submit themselves to God, and those in authority over them. Their heart's desire is an ever-deepening intimacy with the Lord, and they have committed their lives to the service of His Kingdom. They are generous and open-handed, and have a high respect, honour and desire to bless the larger Body of Christ. The Arnotts are able to look beyond the wrinkles in others' theologies and ministry practices, and receive and bless what the Lord is doing in and through flawed human beings like themselves.

They have based the growth of the local church on a conference model of ministry, and they have an implicit love – and stamina!!! – for the conduct of this style of ministry. The Arnotts, and the pastoral staff at the Airport Vineyard, have tried to live out their mission statement, 'To walk in God's love and give it away', and they have more than demonstrated their commitment to sharing that which they've received . . . but none of this answers the question definitively. Nor could it; nor should it.

If it could be reduced to a set of preconditions and a set of transferable principles, a 'methodology', the dynamics of impetus and control would be compromised, even corrupted. The initiative, every night, is the Lord's; it is His sovereign authority, His sovereign choosing to 'visit' the Airport and pour out His Spirit.

To continue to ask 'why?' is to press into the heart of the Incarnation. A biblical foundation for the visitation is the subject of the following chapter.

CHAPTER THREE

EXPANDING OUR OPERATIVE THEOLOGIES

A Biblical Foundation for Renewal and Revival

I pray that the God of our Lord Jesus Christ, the all-glorious Father, may confer on you the spiritual gifts of wisdom and vision, with the knowledge of Him that they bring. I pray that your inward eyes may be enlightened, so that you may know what is the hope to which He calls you, how rich and glorious is the share He offers you among His people in their inheritance, and how vast are the resources of His power open to us who have faith . . . (Ephesians 1:17–19)

Somewhere around 20 June, six months after the initial outpouring, first-time attendance at the nightly meetings passed the 50,000 mark. About the same time, the meetings started to catch the attention of the secular media – beginning, oddly enough, in Britain. The first report was filed in the London *Sunday Telegraph*, and then the BBC. Shortly thereafter, Toronto television news stations CFTO and CBC featured spots on the six o'clock news, followed by articles in the Toronto newspaper *The Globe and Mail, The Hamilton Spectator,* and the international *Time Magazine.*[1] By and large, the reports put the renewal in a positive light; the *Globe's* headline, for instance read: 'Revival Church – people are flocking to join a congregation that breaks into laughter, falls to the ground, and roars like a lion.' What was particularly refreshing was that for a change, the secular news had the opportunity to put a church in the spotlight, and for reasons other than scandal.

That needs a qualifier – for reasons other than *moral scandal*. If the New Testament word *scandalon* is pressed into service, the meetings at the Airport have about them the 'scandalous' – they are, as *scandalon* is usually translated, somewhat of a 'stumbling block' to some. As was noted in the preceding chapter, it's completely impossible to document how many have come to their first service, watched for a while, and left, having drawn the conclusion that what they were witnessing 'wasn't God'.

That reaction is not untypical, for it has both biblical and historical precedent, so much so that it can be said, 'there never yet was any great manifestation that God made of Himself to the world, without many difficulties attending it.'[2] Several aspects come to bear here – primarily our personal experiences and expectations. They, in turn, hinge on our understanding of what, theologically speaking, is known as the *manifest presence* of God, those times and occasions when God makes His

[1] CFTO, Friday, 24 June; *Globe*, Wednesday, 6 July; *Spectator*, Saturday, 23 July; *Time*, 15 August, p. 43.
[2] Jonathan Edwards, *The Distinguishing Marks of a Work of the Spirit of God,* in *The Works of Jonathan Edwards,* vol. II, Banner of Truth Trust, Edinburgh, 1992, p.273a.

presence known, when we are allowed and enabled to 'see, hear, or feel' His presence with us.

One of the newspaper stories articulates this with precision; though it was written as a catchy tag to the article, there is, nevertheless, profound theological astuteness in the following words: 'British Airways flight #092 took off from Toronto Airport on Thursday evening just as the Holy Spirit was landing on a small building a hundred yards from the end of the runway.'[3] Many both inside and out of the Church read that, and scoffed, yet it is a declaration with penetrating biblical insight.

Theologians speak of God's *presence* in two ways; He is '*omnipresent*'. That is to say, God is in every place, at every time. It's a conceptual thing, a philosophical, intellectual belief; it has to do with God's 'BIGNESS'; it's rather difficult to be the Supreme Being, the Creator and Master of the Universe, and NOT be omnipresent.

It's also a declaration of *faith,* one that's based on biblical revelation. One example will suffice: in Psalm 139, verse 7, the question is asked, 'Where can I go from Your Spirit, where can I flee from Your Presence?' The Psalmist is reflecting on God's 'everywhere-ness'.[4] God's *omnipresence,* every moment, at all times, in every place.

[3] The *Sunday Telegraph*, London.

[4] In this case, it might be more accurate to say, he is *lamenting* the Lord's omnipresence, given the context of the Psalm!

Writing 500 years ago, the German mystic Meister Eckhart put it this way: 'There is no place that God isn't'; Martin Luther simply said: 'God is closer to everything than anything is to itself'.

The thing is, God's omnipresence is a rather abstract, intangible concept. As the Psalmist knew, it isn't exactly *comforting* in a *personal* kind of way. God's omnipresence is an essential frame, or context, or backdrop for the living of our faith, but it's not a dynamic that radically changes our lives.

In pressing towards an understanding of the second way of describing God's presence, we've attempted to do a bit of an informal survey at the Airport Vineyard, and, on occasion, asked, 'If you relied *only* on your *personal,* subjective and *RECENT* experience, how many of you would, without reservation, conclude that God is VERY near, and intimately present to you?'

Some nod 'Yes'. They have recently experienced the presence of the Lord, and they're so sure of the encounter, the revelation, the 'touch', there is absolutely no doubt in their minds. Some of them have *seen* the Lord, or something of His glory; there has been given to them a dream or an open vision. Some of them have *heard* audible words; some have heard words only with their hearts, but words, none the less; words that left them with no doubt as to Who pronounced them. Some have *felt* the Lord's touch, physically. Some have felt the Lord's healing hand upon them, or the hand of blessing. Not until I came to the Airport had I heard of anyone *smelling* the presence of God, but having personally ministered on an occasion where that was the case, that's part of the experience of the presence of God too!

There is long, and strong *biblical* precedent for this kind of direct, personal encounter with God; the Scriptures are, in fact, the extended chronicling of the times, occasions and seasons when God has made known His presence – to Adam and Eve, to Abraham, to Moses and Israel . . . to the prophets . . . at Pentecost, and at the conversion of Saul – to hit but a few of the 'high-water marks'. The entire Bible is a declaration of God's dynamic presence in the midst of His people, whether it be a celebration of His intervention in the past, a chronicling of recent experience, or an anticipation of His ultimate and eternal manifestation at the end of history when 'God Himself will be with His people.' (Revelation 21:3). Start to finish, the Scriptures are a literary record of God's coming to humankind, at His initiative. It is the *experiential* reality of the presence of God that stands at the centre of biblical faith; the 'theology of presence' is so much the unique feature of the Scriptures, that it is that which distinguishes Christian faith from both classical antiquity, and current world religions.[5]

And God has not JUST made Himself known in biblical times and then disappeared; there is continuous and documented evidence of His disclosure throughout the history of the Church.

[5] Samuel Terrien, *The Elusive Presence: the Heart of Biblical Theology*, Harper and Row, New York, 1978, pp. xxviii and 28.

Thomas Aquinas stands as one of the intellectual giants of Christendom; his imprint on matters of dogmatic and moral theology, philosophy and exegesis is formidable. Current editions of his work fill twenty-five volumes, averaging 650 pages each. To represent his work in the space of a paragraph is inconceivable; one provocative citation will stand alone: 'Sheer joy is God's, and this demands companionship.'[6]

Near the end of his life, early in December 1273, while saying Mass, Aquinas was so moved, that he neither dictated nor wrote another word. So untypical was this that one of his personal secretaries urged him to resume his work, to which the great Doctor replied, 'I can't. Everything I have written seems like straw in comparison with what I have seen and what has been revealed to me.'[7]

The mathematician, physicist, philosopher and theologian, Blaise Pascal documented an experience of God's presence that so profoundly influenced him, he kept his transcript of it with him, sewn in the lining of his jacket. He titled the account, *The Memorial.*

> In the year of grace, 1654, on Monday, 23 November
> . . . from about half past ten in the evening until about half past twelve,
> *FIRE.*

[6] Thomas Aquinas, *Commentary on the Book of Sentences by Peter Lombard,* 1 Sent. 2.1.4.

[7] *Albert and Thomas, Selected Writings,* ed. Simon Tugwell, Paulist Press, New York, 1988, p.266.

God of Abraham, God of Isaac, God of Jacob, not of the philosophers and scholars.
Certitude. Certitude. Feeling. Joy. Peace.
God of Jesus Christ.
Deum meum et Deum vestrum (My God and Your God) . . .
Joy, joy, joy, tears of joy . . .
Let me never be separated from Him.
We keep hold of Him only by the ways taught in the Gospel.
Renunciation, total and sweet.
Total submission to Jesus Christ . . .
Eternally in joy for a day's training on earth.[8]

David Brainerd was a pioneer missionary to the Indians of New England. His *Diary,* edited and published by Jonathan Edwards, was the first biography printed in America to gain international recognition, and was the first full missionary biography ever published.[9] Brainerd recorded the following experience in his journal:

> In a mournful melancholy state, I was attempting to pray; but found no heart to engage in that or any other duty . . . As I was walking in a dark thick grove, unspeakable glory seemed to open to the view and apprehension of my soul. I do not mean any external

[8] Blaise Pascal, *Pensées*, trans. A. Krailsheimer, Penguin Books, London 1966, p. 309.
[9] Iain Murray, *Jonathan Edwards: A New Biography,* Banner of Truth Trust, Edinburgh, 1987, p. 307.

> brightness, for I saw no such thing; nor do I intend any imagination of a body of light, somewhere in the third heavens, or any thing of that nature; but it was a new inward apprehension or view that I had of God, such as I never had before, nor any thing which had the least resemblance of it. I stood still; wondered; and admired! I knew that I never had seen before any thing comparable to it for excellency and beauty; it was widely different from all the conceptions that ever I had of God, or things divine.
>
> My soul rejoiced with joy unspeakable, to see such a God, such a glorious divine Being; and I was inwardly pleased and satisfied, that he should be God over all for ever and ever. My soul was so captivated and delighted with the excellency, loveliness, greatness, and other perfections of God, that I was even swallowed up in Him.[10]

Throughout the history of the Church, it has been the experience of God's 'felt' presence that has called men and women to faith and to mission. Eckhart puts the issue squarely: 'Suppose a man were in hiding, and he stirred himself; he gives his whereabouts thereby. And God does the same; no one could ever have found Him – He gives Himself away.'

[10] *Memoirs of the Rev. David Brainerd, Missionary to the Indians.... by Jonathan Edwards,* in *The Works of Jonathan Edwards,* vol. II, *op. cit.,* p.319b.

Hugh Kerr and John Mulder edit a helpful and accessible collection of documented experiences of the manifest presence of God in their book, *Conversions: the Christian Experience,* Eerdmans, Grand Rapids, Michigan, 1983.

We began with a brief consideration of God's *omnipresence;* the focus of our attention is now the *manifest* presence of God. Not propositional belief, the substance of faith, but personal *experience,* whereby we personally see, hear and feel the immediate nearness of God.

Theologically, what we are talking about is the omnipresent and eternal God *localizing and actualizing His presence,* in space and time. Again, this is absolutely central to our Christian faith: the coming of God, to us. In fact, if we take out of the Scriptures all the references to the manifest presence of God, what we are left with are the genealogies, the Book of Esther, Proverbs and Philemon. We even have to surrender some of *that* when we understand that in the Book of Proverbs, the 'Wisdom of the Lord' is personified – and as such, 'She' comes to meet us.[11] We have virtually no Bible without God making Himself known to His people, experientially.

So . . . the *Telegraph* reporter brought theological accuracy to bear when he wrote of 'the Holy Spirit landing at the end of the Toronto runway', such that His presence was known, felt and seen, to those gathered.

The biblical record is full of accounts of people being physically 'moved' when they experience God's immediacy. For instance, Abraham falls to the ground, as

[11] See especially Proverbs 8:1, 4, 6 and17: 'Hear how wisdom calls and understanding lifts her voice . . . It is to you I call . . . Listen, for I shall speak clearly . . . Those who love me I love, and those who search for me will find me.'

do King Saul, the prophet Ezekiel, the soon-to-be Apostle Paul, and the Apostle John. (Genesis 15:12; 1 Samuel 19:24; Ezekiel 3:23; Acts 9:4; Revelation 1:17). However, attempting to *prove* the Scriptural validity of the physical manifestations witnessed at the Airport can have one skating on some pretty thin ice. The counsel offered by the Bible scholar, J.L. McKenzie, seems sufficient: 'If a severe blow to the head can make one see stars, we hesitate to say what a man would see if God spoke to him.'[12]

While not *pre*scriptive, dictating what should or must happen when God's immediate presence is experienced, Daniel 10:4 and following is probably the fullest *des*cription detailed in the Scriptures, of 'God showing up', a favourite Vineyard expression.

> On the twenty-fourth day of the first month, . . . I looked up and saw a man robed in linen . . . his face shone like lightning . . . and when he spoke, his voice sounded like the voice of a multitude. I, Daniel, alone saw the vision; . . . and my strength drained away; and sapped of my strength I became a sorry figure of a man. I heard the sound of his words and as I did so, I lay prone on the ground in a trance. Suddenly, at the touch of a hand, I was set, all trembling, on my hands and knees. 'Daniel, man greatly beloved,' he said to me, 'attend to the words I am about to speak to you . . . Do not be afraid . . .' While he spoke in this

[12] J.L. McKenzie, *The Two-Edged Sword*, Image Books, New York, p.52

> fashion to me, I fixed my eyes on the ground and was unable to speak. Suddenly one with human appearance touched my lips . . . Again the figure touched me and put strength into me, saying, 'Do not be afraid, man greatly beloved; all will be well with you. Take heart, and be strong.' As he spoke, my strength returned . . . (Daniel 10:4, 6, 7-12, 15-16, 18-19).

The conclusion of this encounter is prophetic revelation and a re-commissioning.

Night after night, there are countless testimonies of those who have experienced aspects of the outlined phenomena – falling, shaking, trembling; the seeing of visions unseen by others; hearing words spoken, often of consolation, encouragement and announcement as to future ministry plans; people have heard their names called, and felt the 'touch' of the Lord's hand upon them. Longstanding fears have been lifted, and a sense of hope has been 'revived', such that many are at a loss for words to describe the transformation they feel.

Further, thousands have pressed into the experiential reality of biblical calls to 'take delight in the Lord'; to 'rejoice greatly', to 'shout for joy'. The laughter that often overtakes the meetings is but one expression of this joy in the Lord.

The question has been raised repeatedly, 'Why all of this, all of a sudden?' One answer is found in writing a history of 'season' to describe God's relationship with His people, times of new growth – a springtime season; times of rich fruitfulness – summer; times of silence, stillness, even death – fall and winter. As it is recorded in the Old Testament, Israel's experience certainly reflects this cyclical movement, from bondage to liberty in the exodus from Egypt, and back again to desert wanderings . . . through to the 'springtime' reforms and 'summertime' revivals under Elijah after long seasons of fall and winter; similar seasons of redemption under the kings, Jehoshaphat, Hezekiah, and Josiah; or Ezra and Nehemiah. (See Exodus 19; 1 Kings 18; 2 Chronicles 20; 2 Chronicles 30; 2 Chronicles 34-35; Ezra 3 and 6; Nehemiah 8 respectively). Psalm 85 verse 6 puts forth the cry: 'Will You not revive us again, that Your people may rejoice in You?' The spirit of that call for renewal is issued repeatedly – Psalm 126 reflects this 'seasonality'; it begins with a time referent 'when', and verse 4 sounds a request that the Lord bring the season of restoration again:

> When the Lord restored the fortunes of Zion,
> we were like people renewed in health.
> Our mouths were full of laughter
> and our tongues sang aloud for joy . . .
> Restore our fortunes Lord,
> as streams return in the dry south.
> Those who sow in tears
> will reap with songs of joy . . .

In the Book of Acts, the Apostle Peter speaks of 'times of recovery', or interpretively, that 'refreshing may come from the presence of the Lord' (Acts 3:19, . . .). All of this is even more firmly grounded in Jesus' announcement text: 'The time has arrived; the Kingdom of God is upon you. Repent and believe the gospel' (Mark 1.14–15).

Time is a key word here, because in biblical Greek, there are two words for 'time': the first is *chronos;* English words like chronometer and chronology are derived from its root. *Chronos* is clock time, calendar time: 1 o'clock, 2 o'clock, 3 o'clock; January, February, March . . . all marching right along.

The second Greek word, *kairos* is special time. Those who are mothers know the difference between *chronos* and *kairos.* About nine months or so into a pregnancy – *chronos* time – many soon-to-be mothers shake their husband by the shoulder and say . . . 'It's *time!*' He opens a bleary eye, looks at the clock, and says, 'It's 3.17 in the morning; go back to sleep!'

She's on *kairos* time, he's talking *chronos.* So he gets shaken again: 'IT'S **TIME**!!!' And this time he gets it. !!!'IT'S **TIME!!!!**'

Kairos time has a connotation of 'pregnancy' about it; something is always brought to birth. In the Gospel of Mark, what's brought to birth is the presence and the power of the Kingdom of God, made known in Jesus, in His preaching and His ministry. That the time has 'arrived', or 'is fulfilled', speaks of something that has come to term, been brought to completion; its final stage is now present reality. It is not *almost* or nearly 'delivery time'; IT'S **TIME!!!**

In Jesus is the commencement of the future that God had announced through the prophets of old. This is declared by Jesus when he reads from the scroll of Isaiah 61, and concludes that 'today, in your hearing, this text has come true'. That the words 'this day', are emphatic implies that the prophetically announced time of fulfilment has begun, in Jesus.[13]

This has strong complement in Matthew's announcement of the Gospel, chapters 1:21 and 23, and 2:1-6. We're so familiar with the Christmas story, that these seem 'sleeper texts'; they reflect, nevertheless, the very core of Christian faith. In these texts in Matthew's Gospel, what is born is, literally, Jesus. His name? *Emmanuel*. Perfect Hebrew for 'God is with us'. As such, Jesus is the *ultimate* manifestation of God's Presence.

Unpacking these verses and their context gives us firm footing to understand and discern the 'visitation' at the Airport Vineyard.

Jesus is 'born of a virgin', but 'conceived by the Spirit'. There is a 'host' for the manifestation of God's presence, but the focal issue here is that of the *initiative* for the birthing. It is ALWAYS God's, always the case with the manifest presence, for it is NEVER something we cook up or contrive. It is always gift. Pure grace. Something *given*.

Why would God visit His people, either in Jesus, or by

[13] Luke 4:21; see Herman Ridderbos, *The Coming of the Kingdom*, trans. H. de Jongste, The Presbyterian and Reformed Publishing Company, Philadelphia, 1962, p. 49. See also Matthew 12:28, Luke 11:20; Luke 10:9-11; Luke 10:23-26; 11:31-32; Matthew 11:46, 12.

His Spirit in subsequent visitations? Matthew makes this crystal clear: chapter 1:21: 'He will save His people from their sins.' The heart of God is to make right what we've made wrong. His gracious purpose is to give us a new start; to renovate – better, *to restore.*

The restoration, however, is not just forgiveness, though a huge slice of Christendom has settled for that much and no more. There is the Lord's 'Emmanuel-ness'; in Matthew's Gospel, there is a completed loop – be it in human form, or Resurrected presence, the Lord Jesus 'will be with us always' (Matthew 1:23 and 28:20).

Matthew tells us what the Lord's presence means: He comes as 'a ruler to be shepherd' (Matthew 2:6). That declaration is almost a contradiction in terms, given the world's values system – power and compassion do not typically co-habitate. It is, however, what is at the root of all of the physical manifestations that have the Airport hopping. What is being imparted is a fresh revelation of the Lord's authority of care over people's lives, His shepherd's rule.

Most of us aren't from farming backgrounds; fortunately, we have a first-hand description of what a shepherd's care is like, in Psalm 23. Those who've done 'carpet time' at the Airport have a frame of reference for much of what is declared in the Psalm, not least being the dynamic of verse 2: 'He *makes* me lie down . . .'! That, and a new sense of the Lord's 'sufficiency', such that we 'want for nothing'; of the Lord 'restoring our souls', of 'guidance and counsel for His name's sake', 'comfort and consolation, even in the darkest valleys of our lives', of 'PARTYING at His banqueting table' . . . the graphic descriptions of the Psalm have new experiential content for thousands upon thousands.

A final gleaning from Matthew's announcement text: the wise ones seek out the revelation of God's manifest presence, whatever the cost. Often, it is an issue of dignity. The wise men who came from the east to pay homage were not too proud to worship a newborn baby, in an out-of-the-way little village in Judea. Nor are those who seek out 'the Holy Spirit's landing at the end of an airport runway'. Who would have figured? It seems that our expectations typically get assaulted. Just as the King of the Jews was not found in the Holy Temple or even the Holy City, even so, God has chosen to manifest His presence, not in a cathedral or sanctuary, but in an industrial unit, a place that doesn't look even remotely like a church building. The smart ones are willing to travel when the Spirit of God is manifested.

A curious manifestation has been exhibited at the Airport meetings, and noted elsewhere.[14] Those affected jump up and down in one spot, sometimes for extended periods of

[14] See John White's *When the Spirit Comes with Power*, p. 94; in meetings conducted by Daniel Rowland, a revival preacher in Wales (1762) it was reported that 'the bodies of two or three, sometimes ten or twelve, are violently agitated, and they leap up and down in all manner of postures, frequently for hours together.' Eifon Evans, *Daniel Rowland and the Great Awakening in Wales*, Banner of Truth Trust, 1985, p. 317.

time. Not surprisingly, the phenomenon has been dubbed 'pogoing'. To my knowledge, there is no Biblical parallel, or basis for such a physical manifestation of the Spirit's power and presence on a person. Does that mean that it is necessarily 'of the flesh?' Should pogo-ers be taken aside immediately, and corrected?

Such a commitment to rigid biblical literalism is not conducive to the Spirit of revival. Suffice it to say that there is little by way of a biblical basis to 'prove' the validity of ANY particular physical manifestation. There is, however, clear counsel to 'test the spirits'. (1 John 4:1ff). That test lies, not so much on what is happening physically, on the 'outside' of the pogo-er, but spiritually, on the 'inside'. One of the key tests is a simple, but subjective one: having bounced, or better, *been* bounced, does the person love Jesus more?

If we understand that fundamental to Christian faith is a call to intimate relationship with God in Christ, then an essential dynamic of the maturing of our relationship with God is an ever-deepening intimacy with the Lord. Even a quick survey demonstrates God's desires in this regard. In Genesis 3.8-9, the Lord asks after Adam and Eve, 'Where are you?' It was not that the omnipresent and omniscient Lord needed to know where they were; after their sin, *they* needed to declare themselves; they needed to get found. The Lord's question offered them the opportunity to work towards restoration.

Throughout the Old Testament, there are several phrases used for God's 'showing up': the Lord simply 'appears'; He 'descends'; He 'shows Himself'. However, biblical Hebrew does not possess an abstract word meaning *presence.* The word *panim* 'face', as in the expression *the face of Yahweh,* is the most common phrase for the experience of the manifest presence of the Lord. That, because the experience of God's immediate presence is not theoretical abstraction, but relational reality, the foundational grounding for the covenants – 'I will be Your God, and you shall be My people.'

It was said of Moses, for instance, 'that the Lord used to speak with him face to face, as one man speaks to another.'[15] Aaron's priestly blessing, in Numbers 6:20, is the calling forth of this same intimacy:

> May the Lord bless you and guard you;
> may the Lord *make His face shine upon you*
> and be gracious to you;
> may the Lord look kindly on you
> and give you peace.

The blessing is not a 'stand alone'; it is a repeated intercession, especially in the Psalms: the refrain in Psalm 80 is perhaps the best example: 'God of Hosts, restore us, and *make Your face to shine upon us,* that we might be saved.' (Psalm 80:3, 7, 19; see also Psalms 27:8; 67:1; 119:135). The call is issued to the faithful that they are to 'look to the Lord and be strong; at all times *seek His face.*' (1

[15] Exodus 33:11. It should be noted that later in that same chapter, verses 18 and following, Moses asks to see the Lord's *glory*. It is in this context, in asking for an *even fuller revelation* than he has previously seen, that Moses is told that 'no mortal can see My face and live' (Exodus 33:20). Moses must be 'shielded' from the full revelation of the Lord's glory when He passes by, verses 21-23.

Chronicles 16:11; Psalm 105:4). God's people are in agony, even to the point of despairing of life, when experiencing the sensed *absence* of God:

> How long, Lord, will You leave me forgotten,
> how long hide Your face from me?
> How long must I suffer anguish in my soul, grief in my heart day after day? . . .
> Lord, answer me soon;
> my spirit faints.
> Do not hide Your face from me
> or I shall be like those who go down to the abyss.
> (Psalms 13:1–2 and 147:7; see also Psalms 27:8–9; 30:7; 51:9; 69:17; 88:14; 102:2; 104:29; 104:29).

The prophets continually warn that Israel's unfaithfulness will necessarily cause the Lord to withdraw His manifest presence: 'The Lord's arm is not too short to save, nor His ear too dull to hear; rather, it is your iniquities that raise a barrier between you and Your God; it is your sins that veil His face.' (Isaiah 59:1–2; see also Psalm 34:16). The Lord Himself makes solemn decrees that His sensed presence is, in part, dependent on the people's singleness of heart: 'I shall set my face against anyone who wantonly resorts to mediums and spirits . . . Consecrate yourselves and be holy, for I the Lord am the Lord Your God.' (Leviticus 20:6; see also Leviticus 20:3; Deuteronomy 31:17–18; 32:20).

Because of the Lord's holiness, glory and majesty, it is not untypical that when someone sees His face, they characteristically end up on theirs! For instance, Jacob –

no paradigm of virtue – is amazed that he had seen God face to face, and yet his life had been spared. (Genesis 32:30). He carries the physical results of that meeting in his body for the rest of his life. Abraham, Ezekiel, Daniel, and John the Apostle, all end up face first.(Genesis 17:3, 17; 1:28; 43:3; 44:4; Daniel 8:18; 10:9; Revelation 1:17). But the mystery of Judeo-Christian faith rests in the fact that Creator and Master of the Universe, the Holy One, desires relationship. The promise that comes through the prophet Jeremiah is nothing short of miraculous:

> I alone know My purpose for you, says the Lord: wellbeing and not misfortune, and a long line of descendants after you. If you invoke Me and come and pray to Me, I shall listen to you: when you seek Me, you will find Me; if you search wholeheartedly, I shall let you find Me, says the Lord. I shall restore your fortunes; I shall gather you from all the nations . . . (Jeremiah 29:11–14).

Intimacy with God. By definition, the innermost, closest, deepest *knowing.* Communion – co-union. The very purpose for which we were designed . . . and most of us don't know very much about what it means to be intimate with anyone! We've spent the balance of our lives building and then living behind protective personal walls.

But God calls us out! From start to finish, from Genesis, 'Where are you?' to Revelation, 'Come!', God calls us out.

The Lord knows where we are; the question the Bible asks of us is, do we?

This chapter began with a consideration of the scandalous, the stumbling block. For Jesus, in controversy after controversy with the Pharisees, the centre of concern is that of *intimacy* with the Father, the One whom He knew as *Abba:* 'Daddy.'

As Jesus revealed the Father, as He talked about Him and His Kingly rule and demonstrated His purposes, what is unquestionably revealed is a relationship of intimacy, not formality. In Jesus, there is a unique consciousness of God's presence, such that Jesus mandates the conduct of His ministry on the grounds of direct communication with the Father. Repeatedly, He justifies His actions with words to this effect: 'In very truth I tell you, the Son can do nothing by Himself; He does only what He sees the Father doing: whatever the Father does, the Son does.' (John 5:19; see also Matthew 11:25-27; John 8:38; 12:49-50). His indictment of the Pharisees is just the opposite, that they have no intimacy with God:

> His voice you have not heard, His form you have never seen; His word has found no home in you, because you do not believe the One whom He sent. You study the Scriptures diligently, supposing that in them you have eternal life; their testimony points to Me, yet you refuse to come to Me to receive that life. (John 5:37-40).

This is not the case for those who follow Jesus, be they the first of His disciples, or the generations that come after. In the Lord's final instructions to His disciples before His death, Jesus makes it clear that His purpose in coming was to share with His followers the same intimacy that He knew with the Father. Jesus tells them that Another Revealer, the Comforter, will also make known the Father. (John 14:26; 16:13-15). It is this experiential intimacy with the Father that is the very heart of the Lord's priestly prayer for the disciples:

> Righteous Father, although the world does not know You, I know You, and they know that You sent Me. I made Your name known to them, and will make it known, *so that* the love You had for Me may be in them, and I in them. (John 17:25-26).

In turning from the intimacy that Jesus had with God, to the experiences of the early Christian community, I went looking for help. One of the most important books I've ever read is James G.D. Dunn's, *Jesus and the Spirit*. I've used my copy so often, and so hard, it has to be held together with a shoelace; I worked through it again, looking for direction in discerning what was happening at the Airport Vineyard.

Dunn begins his study by asking what it is that qualifies as 'religious experience'. If we answer that it is a recognition of a manifestation of the presence of God in a person's life, the questions then have to be asked, *What do we mean by THAT?* and, *How do we distinguish such an experience of God from other physiological, or sociological, or darker – demonic forces – at work?*[16] These questions are *key*, given the unusual and dynamic 'religious experiences' many are having at the Airport Vineyard!

Dunn issues a caution at the start of his work, for he recognizes an implicit ambiguity to religious experience; WHAT a person experiences, HOW he or she describes it, and WHAT can be proved either by way of that experience's source or consequence . . . is impossible to prove scientifically. Recognizing this fact, Dunn calls for an investigative openness:

> We must be aware of prejudicing the range of religious experience which is 'proper' or of religious value. Christian theology has often attempted to reduce Christian experience in effect to a rather bare 'feeling of dependence', or to the moral earnestness of the categorical imperative, and has withdrawn in ill-concealed horror from more extravagant manifestations of religious feeling . . .
>
> [But] some of the more extravagant manifestations of religious experience played not an unimportant role in earliest Christianity.[17]

Understanding that the Gospels were not written as critical history, or even theology, but rather, as the early Church's witness of the *experience* of Jesus and His Spirit,

[16] James G.D. Dunn, *Jesus and the Spirit*, SCM Press, 1983, p.1.
[17] *Ibid.*, p.3

we begin to read familiar texts with new eyes, and see things we perhaps never saw before. Luke, for instance, makes it very clear that the early Church experienced a spiritual vitality such that they lived and breathed the miraculous.

Birthed at Pentecost, the early Church concluded that what was foretold by the prophet Joel was now fulfilled, in the presence of the Risen Lord Jesus (Joel 2:28f). What they experienced – the hearing of the rushing wind; the corporate vision of tongues of fire; the ecstatic language; the outrageous, even incapacitating joy – followed by even further signs and wonders led them to conclude that they were now *filled* with His Spirit. (Acts 2:4; 6:3,5,8; 7:55; 11:24). Together they experienced a pervasive sense of the Lord's presence and power, the fulfilment of the promises Jesus made to them before His death and before His ascension: 'I will be with you always' (John 14:18; 15:4; Matthew 28:20).

The living out of these promises is seen in a verse such as Acts 14:3: 'Paul and Barnabas stayed on for some time, and spoke boldly and openly in reliance on the Lord, who confirmed the message of His grace by enabling them to work signs and miracles.' Here Luke describes the aspects of charismatic fellowship and complement – Paul and Barnabas working *together*; a boldness and freedom in proclaiming the Gospel; an unapologetic dependence upon the Lord for power and authority; and a confirmation of their 'word' about Jesus through the demonstration of the 'works' of Jesus. (See also Acts 2:42-47; 4:29-31; 5:12; 6:8; 8:6; 13; 11:23; 13:52; 15:12).

Further, the worship of the early Church is characterized by an openness to, and a dependence on, the immediate inspiration of the Spirit, be it through prophecy, spontaneous prayer and extemporaneous preaching, spiritual songs, and perhaps above all, an unfettered enthusiasm and joy. (Acts 2:46; Philippians 4:4; 1 Peter 1:6, 8). This is one of the striking features of the community life and worship of the early Church; so much so, that Johannes Weiss remarks:

> A tempestuous enthusiasm, and overwhelming intensity of feeling, an immediate awareness of the presence of God, an incomparable sense of power and an irresistible control over the will and inner spirit and even the physical condition of other men – these are ineradicable features of historic early Christianity . . . . Unless one can understand this constant mood of victorious, jubilant happiness and confidence, he simply will not understand primitive Christianity.[18]

As Dunn works through his analysis of the 'enthusiastic beginnings' of the early Church, he boldly raises the following questions:

> Were any of the physical or psychical manifestations regarded as a particular sign of the Spirit, a *necessary* proof of the Spirit's presence? – glossolalia, prophecy, healings, visions, or more generally, eschatological

[18] Johannes Weiss, *Earliest Christianity, Harper, 1959,* p.41.

> enthusiasm, inspired worship, charismatic authority? The question is one which has troubled Christianity more or less from the first . . .
>
> The earliest Christian community was essentially charismatic and enthusiastic in nature, in every aspect of its common life and worship, its development and mission . . . The fact is that ecstatic and physical phenomena have been a regular concomitant of religious awakening and revival movements within the history of Christianity . . . Not for nothing were the Quakers and Shakers so nicknamed.[19]

When the Book of Acts is reviewed, it is incontestable that there is a remarkable diversity of charismatic spiritual experience represented in the early communities, and that it is so rich in its variety that it defies standardization, form and formula, and sometimes even interpretation! It was these *experiences* of spiritual encounter, of visions, revelations, commissions, signs, wonders, and the other manifestations of the Spirit's presence and power that were the source and impetus for the mission in which the early Church engaged. Their worship, proclamation, evangelism, and care ministries were all grounded in the dynamic encounter with the Spirit of the Risen Christ.

The world in which supernatural forces are at work, often with visible, tangible and bodily effect, is distasteful, even repulsive for some. Throughout the history of the

[19] Dunn, *op. cit.*, pp. 189, 194 and 192.

Church, such 'enthusiasts' have been ostracized, condemned or worse. The description, however, fits the religious experience of the early Church following Pentecost.

This fact is even more firmly established when we consider the declarations the Apostle Paul makes of his spiritual experience and ministry. Again, what we conclude is dependent on what has the focus of our attention. If we ask – how is the Spirit of the Risen Christ to be at work in a person's *life*? How is the Spirit of the Risen Christ to be at work in a community's midst? What is it going to look like? How will we know when it happens? What do we expect? – questions such as these may open for us whole new arenas . . . it may be something akin to 'crash helmet stuff', to use Annie Dillard's expression, such that we're drawn out to where we can never return.

For the Apostle Paul, his understanding and expectation of the Spirit of the Risen Christ was always *experiential.* It was not *primarily* theological, doctrinal or speculative. The thinking about it all came after, secondarily. First and foremost, it was experiential. His initiating encounter with the Spirit of the Risen Christ literally knocked him off his high horse, struck him blind for a while before he got healed, and certainly drew him out to where *he* could never return. (Acts 9)

His experience of the Spirit was that of power; life-transforming power operating on the heart, the inner centre of being, of thought, and will. The Spirit that is the source of a love that 'floods' the heart with God's love, and causes an irrepressible joy to gush out, such that all other oppositional forces are overcome. In the Spirit, Paul spoke in tongues freely and frequently, worked signs and wonders, received visions and revelations, and laboured with supernatural faith, power, wisdom, authority and boldness. Unashamedly, he himself discloses as much, in passages of his letters that are biographical in content. (1 Corinthians 14:18; 2 Corinthians 3–4; 6:3–13; 11 and 12; Galatians 1:11–2:2).

In terms of the proclamation of the Gospel, Paul contrasts his preaching with rhetoric. In 1 Corinthians 2:4 and following, he differentiates 'clever arguments' and 'demonstration of Spirit and power', so that 'faith might be built not on human wisdom but on the power of God'. The issue is not rational persuasion, but life-engaging encounter – God's grace coming to visible expression.[20] When he writes to the Church at Thessalonica, he rehearses their experience: 'When we brought you the Gospel we did not bring it in mere words but in the power of the Holy Spirit and with strong conviction.' (1 Thessalonians 1:5). It is not new head-knowledge that brought transformation to the Corinthians and Thessalonians, but the impartation of grace.

Implicitly, he is giving witness to the experiential reality of being *grasped*. Grabbed. Zapped. Wowed. Awed. Overwhelmed. The demonstration of the Gospel

[20] Dunn, *op. cit.*, p. 254.

is not due to Paul's ability as a preacher, a spell-binding speaker with intellectual powers of persuasion – the demonstration of the Gospel has to do with God manifesting His presence and the realities of His Kingdom, speaking truth that calls us out, freeing us up, blessing, healing and forgiving. Releasing things like joy, and peace, and hope and love. *Restoring LIFE.* To that end, Paul intercedes for the Church at Ephesus:

> I pray that the God of our Lord Jesus Christ, the all-glorious Father, may confer on you the spiritual gifts of wisdom and vision, with the knowledge of Him that they bring. I pray that your inward eyes may be enlightened, so that you may know what is the hope to which He calls you, how rich and glorious is the share He offers you among His people in their inheritance, and how vast are the resources of His power open to us who have faith . . . (Ephesians 1:17-19).

It is in prayer, especially, that there comes the fundamental revelation, and impartation, of the Father-heart of God, such that the believer experiences the same intimacy with God as did Jesus. Paul holds up the *apprehension* of this relational intimacy as the purpose, the intention, the end for which the Spirit is given:

> The Spirit you have received is not a spirit of slavery, leading you back into a life of fear, but a Spirit of adoption, enabling us to cry, 'Abba! Father!' The

Spirit of God affirms to our spirit that we are God's children . . . (Romans 8:15, 26; Galatians 4:6).

Paul is convinced that God not only wants us to *be* His children; He wants us to *experience* the reality of this filial relationship as well: 'We have received this Spirit from God . . . so that we may know all that God has lavished upon us.' (1 Corinthians 2:12; Ephesians 3:14-21). Such knowledge is not so much cognitive in nature, not that which is put into notebooks; it is a relational knowing based on the living of life together, hence Paul's call to 'walk by the Spirit', (Romans 8:4; Galatians 5:16 and 25). to be 'led by the Spirit', (Romans 8:14; Galatians 5:18) and be 'filled with the Spirit' (Ephesians 5:18). In the original language of the New Testament, Greek, the verbs are present duratives, and as such, call forth customary, habitual action; these directives call forth ongoing, vital, existential interaction; they imply that we are to *keep on* walking . . . *keep on* being led . . . and *keep on being filled.* So . . . MORE LORD!!!

The Apostle Paul gives extended counsel regarding the 'manifestation of the Spirit' in 1 Corinthians chapter 12. Paul is giving instruction regarding the ways in which God's grace in Jesus Christ is made known. *Charis,* the Greek word for 'grace', and *charismata,* 'grace gifts', are both concrete, specific, and actual experiences in the life and ministry of the early Church. Paul says that in every believer, 'the Spirit is *seen* to be at work for some useful purpose.' Literally, each believer '*manifests* the Spirit' (1 Corinthians 12:7). He is speaking of recognizable actions energized by divine power; for Paul, grace and grace giftings are divine energy which accomplish a particular result, in and through an individual, for the good of the community. A '*manifestation of the Spirit*' discloses and makes known the presence and power of the Spirit – the Spirit *reveals* Himself in the charismata . . . Certain kinds of actions and utterances demonstrate the Spirit's presence and activity, and Paul lists some of them: the gifts of wisdom and knowledge, the gift of faith, gifts of healing, the grace of miraculous powers, prophecy, discernment, speaking in tongues, and interpretation. (1 Corinthians 12:8-11). Because these types of things are taking place in Corinth, the Spirit's presence and power is disclosed, made known, *manifested*.[21]

So, too, is 'the flesh'. For all that was charismata demonstrated in Corinth, there was a carnality that has no recorded equal in the New Testament. Paul can say both 'there is no single gift you lack', and, 'you are infants in Christ, still requiring milk instead of solid food'. (1 Corinthians 1:7 and 3:1-3). Their immaturity does not dissuade him in his call; he goes to great lengths to bring them to centre: 'Make love your aim, and be eager for the gifts of the Spirit' (1 Corinthians 14:1).

In seeking to evaluate what is taking place at the Airport Vineyard, we must understand that the manifest presence of God IS highly subjective. It IS experiential. It IS,

[21] Dunn, *op. cit.*, pp. 209-13.

often, emotional. And, it IS typically messy. From one perspective, God's spoken commission 'messed up' Abraham's life – it took him to places he NEVER would have gone on his own, and had him doing things he NEVER would have done on his own initiative; the same can be said of Moses, and the prophets – Amos essentially says that the Lord *kidnapped* him one day while he was off minding his sheep.

It messed up things for Saul, the Pharisee. He had the equivalent of a tenured position at the local seminary; his theology was circumscribed and systematic; he knew what he knew, and he knew what wasn't of God when he saw it . . . until he got knocked off his high horse. The manifest presence of the Risen Christ undid him thoroughly!

That's one of the things we need to have settled. As much fun as all of the manifestations are – and church has never been so much fun, the manifest presence of God is a radical life-changer. There is no record in the Scriptures of the Lord manifesting His presence, and people staying the same as before.

The *staus quo* (Latin for 'the mess we're currently in') must be surrendered. Sometimes, that means a shift in our operative theology – particularly what we expect of the Spirit, and worship, and ministry. Often the manifest presence of God messes with our expectations of how things ought to be, especially how things ought to be as we gather as church. Sometimes there's a shift in our life-styles and life focus. Several of the testimonies in Chapter 5 are telling declarations to that end.

When the Spirit manifests His presence, it often, if not always, requires that WE 'lose control'. It often means that we give up OUR plans, our goals and agendas, our figurings for our lives . . . Typically, we get called, *by name,* to embrace the mission, the calling to which the Lord lifts us up. In the course of the Scriptures, the manifestation of the Lord's power and presence goes hand in hand with commission. In Matthew 28:16-20, John 20:21-22 and Acts 1:8, the commissioning of the disciples is the hallmark of the manifestation of presence. The Risen Lord Jesus promises He will be with His disciples always, and releases to them His Spirit. He then employs them: 'Go . . . and make disciples'; 'As the Father sent Me, so I send you . . .'; 'You shall be My witnesses . . .' Further, the Apostle Paul makes it clear, 'the Spirit is manifested in each of us *for some useful purpose.*'

HUMILITY, therefore, is the only appropriate posture to take when God manifests His gracious presence: 'Yes Lord.' Like the prophet Isaiah: 'Here am I Lord, send me.'

The alternative is to risk finding ourselves 'at war with God' (Acts 5:34-39).

CHAPTER FOUR

A WELL-TRAVELLED PATH

Jonathan Edwards and the Experiences of the Great Awakening

> *Lord, I have heard of Your fame, and I stand in awe of Your deeds, O Lord. Renew them in our day, in our time make them known.* (Habakkuk 3:2)

Mid-February, while sitting on the floor during one of the ministry times at the Airport Vineyard, I surveyed the bodies laid out everywhere, and leaned over to a newly-made friend and said, 'All of this makes apple sauce of a fellow's theological applecarts.'

I had come to the meetings with a reasonably broad biblical foundation already laid. The study of personal and corporate spiritual renewal has had the focus of my attention for sixteen years. But indispensable as resources like Dunn's *Jesus and the Spirit* are, I needed further help in processing the manifestations I was witnessing and experiencing. I had served the Baptist church since 1979, but personally had never seen much by way of physical demonstrations of the Spirit's power and presence. I figured it was a significant manifestation if we could get people to lean forward, take out their wallets, and put something in the offering plate. As to weeping and wailing, laughing, shaking and flailing and falling about, I had no frame of reference.

Needing to process what I was experiencing, I read John White's very helpful book, *When the Spirit Comes With Power,* and then by way of further research, followed some of his footnote references. They led me to *The Works of Jonathan Edwards.* Though most would be completely unfamiliar with his writings, some would know of him only by reputation, as the fire-and-brimstone preacher of the 'Sinners in the Hands of an Angry God' sermon. If that's all Edwards is known for, it is most unfortunate, because as in almost all of life, context is everything, and given the balance of his writings, Edwards can be considered the foremost theological architect of the Great Awakening, another remarkable move of God, roughly 250 years ago. Edwards hosted, observed, chronicled, reflected on and evaluated the dynamics of renewal and revival in the church that he pastored in Northampton, Massachusetts, and beyond, as revival spread throughout New England, from 1734 when the first wave hit his home church, through to 1742 when the outpouring seemed to come to an end.

The evolution of his voluminous writings gives telling witness to his growing insights, wisdom and discernment, and as such, Edwards' works stand as one of the most helpful resources available. When studied, what emerges as the resounding note throughout all of his extensive theological writings is his passion for what he called 'practical and vital Christianity', religious knowledge as *experience,* held not in the head but in the heart. Some have gone so far as to describe him as 'an evangelical mystic, a man who knew experimentally the work of God's Spirit in the soul.'[1]

Edwards' work was never abstract theology. He wrote as a pastor, and as one who personally experienced the power of the Spirit's presence throughout his life; for example, in his *Personal Narrative,* we read:

> The first instance, that I remember, of that sort of inward, sweet delight in God and divine things, that I have lived in much since, was on reading those words, 1 Timothy 1:17: *Now unto the King eternal, immortal, invisible, the only wise God, be honour and glory for ever and ever.* As I read the words, there came into my soul, and was as it were diffused through it, a sense of the glory of the Divine being; a new sense, quite different from any thing I ever experienced before (I.xiiia *The Works of Jonathan Edwards*).

This experience comes after an agonizing time of extended depression and melancholy; in his 'Diary', we read entries like: 'This day and yesterday, I was exceedingly dull, dry and dead' (I.xxiva). As was customary at the time, Edwards made numerous 'Resolutions', his 'personal performance goals': Resolution #1 reads, 'That I will do whatsoever I think to be most to the glory of God, and my own good, profit, and pleasure, in the whole of my duration' (I.xxb). He records seventy resolutions, all of them written as a young

[1] *Jonathan Edwards, The Preacher,* Ralph Turnbull, Baker Book House, Grand Rapids, Michigan, 1958, p.154.

man in his early twenties. He also records this reflection:

> Dull. I find, by experience, that, let me make resolutions, and do what I will, it is all nothing, and to no purpose at all, without the motions of the Spirit of God; for if the Spirit of God should be as much withdrawn from me always, as for the week past, notwithstanding all I do, I should not grow, but should languish, and miserably fade away . . . It is to no purpose to resolve, except we depend on the grace of God (I.xxivb).

With Edwards, many have come to testify that it is an ongoing *experience of God's grace* that turns the deadness and melancholy to an 'inward sweet delight'.

Especially for those who only know of Edwards as the preacher of the 'Sinners in the Hands of an Angry God' sermon, the following abstracts tell out the fuller picture of the man's spirit:

> My sense of divine things gradually increased, and became more and more lively, and had more of the inward sweetness (I.xiiib). It was my continual strife, day and night, and constant inquiry, how I should be more holy... to be with God, and to spend my eternity in divine love, and holy communion with Christ (I.xiva). I had then, and at other times, the greatest delight in the Holy Scriptures. Oftentimes in reading it every word seemed to touch my heart. I felt a harmony

between something in my heart, and those sweet and powerful words. I seemed often to see so much light exhibited by every sentence, that I could not get along in reading; often dwelling long on one sentence, to see the wonders contained in it; and yet almost every sentence seemed to be full of wonders (I.xivb). I have had a view, that was for me extraordinary, of the glory of the Son of God, as Mediator between God and man, and His wonderful, great, full, pure, and sweet grace and love, and meek and gentle condescension. As near as I can judge, [this view] continued for about an hour; which kept me the greater part of the time in a flood of tears, and weeping aloud. I felt an ardency of soul to be, what I know not otherwise how to express, emptied and annihilated; to lie in the dust, and to be full of Christ alone; to love Him with a holy and pure love; to trust Him; to live to serve and follow Him; and to be perfectly sanctified and made pure, with a divine and heavenly purity. I have several other times had views very much of the same nature, and which have had the same effects . . . I have, many times, had a sense of the glory of the Third Person in the Trinity, and His office as Sanctifier; in His holy operations, communicating divine light and life to the soul. God in the communications of His Holy Spirit, has appeared as an infinite fountain of divine glory and sweetness; being full, and sufficient to fill and satisfy the soul; pouring forth itself in sweet communications; like the sun in its glory, sweetly and pleasantly diffusing light and life. And I have sometimes an affecting sense of the

> excellency of the word of God as a word of life; as the light of life; a sweet, excellent, life-giving word; accompanied with a thirsting after that word, that it might dwell richly in my heart (I.xlviib).

Even more declarative are the accounts of his wife's experience. Sarah Edwards had, as a young teenager, experienced an 'uncommon discovery of God's excellency', and had often rededicated herself to 'the Lord's service and glory'. Repeatedly, she felt 'overwhelmed, and as it were, swallowed up, in the light and the joy of the love of God.' Nevertheless, she had been subject to 'unsteadiness, and many ups and downs, being under great disadvantages . . . and often subject to melancholy, and at times almost over-borne with it' (I.376b). In the *Memoirs* we read of her spiritual advance. 'At the commencement of this remarkable work of grace, (the first outpouring in 1734) she dedicated herself anew to God . . . and during its progress, as well as afterwards, she experienced a degree of religious enjoyment, not previously known . . . Unusual as it was in degree, it was eminently the religion of joy' (I.xlvib).

Through the summer of 1740, and the following winter of 1741, Sarah enjoyed uncommon times of 'spiritual light and enjoyment', and during the last wave of the revival a year later, there was so much that was 'unusual and striking' that Mr Edwards had her draw up 'an exact statement of it' (I.lxiia). Her detailed narrative begins Tuesday night, 19 January 1742.

Mrs Edwards had been feeling uneasy and unhappy,

'low in grace', as she describes it. While earnestly wrestling with God for 'help and greater holiness', she says she came to 'an unusual submission, and willingness to wait on God, with respect to the time and manner in which He should help me, and wished that He should take His own time, and His own way, to do it.' A beautiful and faith-filled resignation.

So disposed, issues of the Fatherhood of God are impressed upon her mind; she asks herself: 'Why can I say, *Father?* Can I now at this time, with the confidence of a child, and without the least misgiving of heart, call God my Father?' The next day, Romans 8:34-9 came to her mind '. . . Who is it that condemns? . . . What shall separate us from the love of Christ . . .?' From her meditations on this passage, she says,

> I cannot find language to express, how *certain* this appeared – my safety, and happiness, and eternal enjoyment of God's immutable love, seemed as durable and unchangeable as God Himself. Melted and overcome by the sweetness of this assurance, I fell into a great flow of tears, and could not forebear weeping aloud. It appeared certain to me that God was my Father, and Christ my Lord and Saviour, that He was mine and I was His. Under a delightful sense of the immediate presence and love of God, these words seemed to come over and over in my mind, 'My God, my all; my God, my all.' The presence of God was so near, and so real, that I seemed scarcely conscious of anything else (I.lxiiia).

> I continued in a very sweet and lively sense of divine things, day and night, sleeping and waking, until Saturday, 23 January (I.lxiiib).

Four days without a break!

> 'The next day, I enjoyed a sweet, and lively, and assured sense of God's infinite grace, and favour, and love to me . . .'

Monday was a little quieter.

> On Tuesday, 'I remained in a sweet and lively exercise of this resignation, and love to and rest in God, seeming to be in my heart from day to day, far above the reach of every thing here below.'

Wednesday night, the church in Northampton was hosting protracted revival meetings. Mrs Edwards was so filled with the grace of God that it 'took away her bodily strength.'[2] She writes: 'I *continued* to have clear views of the future world, of eternal happiness and misery . . .' She and some friends had to stay at the church about three hours after the meeting was dismissed, because most of the time, her 'bodily strength was overcome . . .'

The next day, Mr Buell, a guest preacher in Mr Edwards' absence, was talking with some other guests at

[2] The expressions 'took away my bodily strength', 'overbear the body', and 'fainting' seem to be eighteenth-century equivalents to the falling, resting and 'slain' experiences witnessed at the Airport Vineyard.

the parsonage. Sarah joined them in their conversation on divine goodness, but not for long; 'the intenseness of my feelings again took away my bodily strength' (I.lxiva). Later that day, she says:

> My mind was so impressed with the love of Christ, and a sense of His immediate presence, that I could with difficulty refrain from rising from my seat and leaping for joy. I continued to enjoy this intense, and lively, and refreshing sense of divine things, accompanied with strong emotions, for nearly an hour; after which, I experienced a delightful calm, and peace and rest in God, until I retired for the night; and during the night, both waking and sleeping, I had joyful views of divine things . . . I awoke in the morning of Thursday, 28 January, in the same happy frame of mind.

She got the family breakfast; about nine o'clock, she had been interceding for their home-town of Northampton with such longing that her 'bodily strength was much weakened'. Two hours later, she 'accidentally' went into the room where Mr Buell was talking to some people about the reviving work of the Spirit; her strength was 'immediately taken away', and she sank down on the spot. They propped her up in a chair and continued with their conversations; again, her strength failed her, and she dropped to the floor; they took her up to bed, where she lay 'for a considerable time, faint with joy, while contemplating the glories of the heavenly world'. We're not told who got lunch ready.

Mrs Edwards does relay that during this time, she 'felt a far greater love to the children of God, than ever before. I seemed to love them as my own soul; and when I saw them, my heart went out towards them, with an inexpressible endearedness and sweetness . . . This was accompanied with a ravishing sense of the unspeakable joys of the upper world' (I.lxva). She was out from noon until four, 'being too much exhausted by emotions of joy, to rise and sit up'. Late that afternoon, she regained enough strength to head off to the meeting, and then returned to bed.

> That night, 28 January, was the sweetest night I ever had in my life. I never before, for so long a time together, enjoyed so much of the light, and rest, and sweetness of heaven in my soul . . . with a continual, constant and clear sense of Christ's excellent and transcendent love, of *His nearness to me, and my dearness to Him*[3]; with an inexpressibly sweet calmness of soul in an entire rest in Him . . . It seemed to be all that my feeble frame could sustain.

That sense of intimacy with Christ lasted all night; Friday, the next day, she reflected:

> I never felt such an entire emptiness of self-love, or any regard to any private, selfish interest of my own. It seemed to me that I had entirely done with myself . . . . The glory of God seemed to be all, and in all, and

[3] Emphasis added.

> to swallow up every wish and desire of my heart (I.lxvb).

About ten o'clock, Mr Sheldon dropped by the house, and said to Mrs Edwards, 'The Sun of Righteousness arose on my soul this morning, before day.' It seems that he'd had a particularly dynamic quiet-time; she grinned and said, 'That Sun has not set upon my soul all this night . . .' She proceeded to tell him of her experience of being 'lost in God'; but in the telling, 'this conversation only served to give me a still livelier sense of the reality and excellence of divine things . . .'; her strength was again taken away, this time with 'great agitation of body'. A quarter of an hour later, her strength 'entirely fails'; she told her guests that she felt chilly, so they carried her over to the fireplace.

> As I sat there, I had a most affecting sense of the mighty power of Christ, which had been exerted in what He had done for my soul, and of the glorious and wonderful grace of God in causing [revival] to return to Northampton. So intense were my feelings, when speaking of these things, that I could not forbear rising up and leaping with joy and exultation (I.lxvia).

The household worshipped a while together, and Mrs Edwards commented on one of the hymns they sang: 'So conscious was I of the joyful presence of the Holy Spirit, I could scarcely refrain from leaping with transports of joy.' This 'happy frame of mind' lasted four hours, and off they went to the afternoon's meeting, during the course of which, Sarah had such an overwhelming sense of the glory of God that she said 'I could scarcely refrain from expressing my joy aloud, in the midst of the service.' She noted: 'This same happy frame of mind continued during the evening, and night, and the next day.'

That evening, a neighbour was so concerned with the power and pervasiveness of her friend's experience, that she expressed her fears that Mrs Edwards should die in ecstasy before Mr Edwards' return! (I.lxvia). Later that same night, while Sarah was having her private devotions, she was meditating on the Farewell Discourses in the Gospel of John, chapters 13–17. She noted: 'My soul was so filled with love to Christ, and love to His people, that I fainted under the intenseness of the feeling.'

Reviving, she went to bed, and slept a little while, and then awoke.

> I had a very lively consciousness of God's being near me . . . and as it were, close by, and the way [to heaven] seemed more open, and the communication more immediate and more free. I lay awake most of the night, with a constant, delightful sense of God's great love and infinite condescension, and with a continual view of God as *near,* and as *my God.* Whether waking or sleeping, there was no interruption, throughout the night, to the views of my soul, to its heavenly light, and divine, inexpressible sweetness.

This time, she noted, 'it was without any agitation or

motion of the body' (I.lxvib). Given all that she had been through, this was more than likely received as gracious respite!

Continuously for three days, Mrs Edwards enjoyed 'the sweet nearness of God'. At one point, she lay in bed wondering 'how the world of mankind could lie and sleep, when there was such a God to praise, and rejoice in.' She said she could 'scarcely forbear calling out to those who were asleep in the house, to arise, and rejoice, and praise God.' 'When I arose on the morning of the Sabbath, I felt a love to all mankind, wholly peculiar in its strength and sweetness, far beyond all that I had ever felt before. The power of that love seemed to be inexpressible' (I.lxviia). The rest of the day, from a purely human point of view, was a washout –

> the reality and excellence of heavenly things was so clear, and the affections they excited so intense, that it overcame my strength, and kept my body weak and faint, the great part of the day, so that I could not stand or go without help. The night also was comforting and refreshing. This delightful frame of mind was continued on Monday . . . (I.lxviia).

That evening,

> 'these words THE COMFORTER IS COME were accompanied to my soul with such conscious certainty, and such intense joy, that immediately it took away my strength, and I was falling to the floor; when some of

those who were near me caught me and held me up' (I.lxvii).

Tuesday, Mr Buell, while eating dinner, began to discourse about the glories of the upper world; Mrs Edwards was 'greatly affected'; she apparently fell face-first into her supper. Wednesday, Mr Clark came by the house, and asked how she felt. She began to describe her experiences, but as she did, she said, 'my former impressions of heavenly and divine things were renewed with so much power, and life, and joy, that my strength all failed me, and I remained for some time faint and exhausted' (I.lxviiia).

The next day, Thursday, there was a discussion of the 'enlivening and joyful influences of the Holy Spirit' going on in the parlour; while Mrs Edwards was listening, 'the joy and transport of the preceding night were again renewed . . . I felt such intense love to Christ, and so much delight in praising Him, that I could hardly forbear leaping from my chair and singing aloud for joy and exultation. I continued thus extraordinarily moved [for two and a half hours]'.

Here the first person narrative ends – Mrs Edwards having described her experiences from Tuesday 19 January to Thursday 4 February – seventeen days in all! There is no indication that her remarkable affections and impressions have come to any kind of conclusion; but rather that her documentation has come to a close. And while the focus of these citations may seem to have been on the various physical manifestations Mrs Edwards experienced, her story was intended to serve as a glowing witness of 'true religion of the heart, the gracious work of God on a soul, THE RICHES OF FULL ASSURANCE.' The issue is not so much the heat of her religious passions, but rather as Edwards assessed it, 'These high transports, *when past*, have had abiding effects in the increase of sweetness, rest, and humility which they have left upon the soul; and a new engagedness of heart to live to the honour of God, and to watch and fight against sin'(I.376b).[4]

Mr Edwards never put into print any direct comment on, or assessment of, his wife's experiences; however, he does use her story anonymously as one with whom he has been familiar in his extended treatise, *Thoughts on Revival.* His detailed description of her experience extends to five and a half pages; in even a brief excerpt, one cannot but note how unashamed he is of the manifestations experienced, nor can one be unimpressed with the evaluation he draws of the fruit of the work.

> I have been particularly acquainted with many persons who have been the subjects of the high and extraordinary transports of the present day. But in the highest transports I have been acquainted with, and where the affections of admiration, love and joy, so far as another could judge, have been raised to the highest pitch, the following things have been united: a very frequent dwelling for some considerable time together,

[4] Emphasis added.

> in views of the glory of the divine perfections and Christ's excellencies, so that the soul has been as it were perfectly overwhelmed, and swallowed up with light and love, a sweet solace, and a rest and joy of soul altogether unspeakable, sometimes for five or six hours together, without interruption ... Extraordinary views of divine things, and the religious affections, were frequently attended with very great effect on the body ... The person was deprived of all ability to stand or speak ... By times the soul has been so overcome with admiration and a kind of omnipotent joy, as to cause the person, unavoidably, to leap with all their might, with joy and mighty exultation.

None of this was due to 'enthusiastic example' – or 'distemper catched from Mr Whitefield' – it began before he was in the country! (I.376a). Nor were these effects on the body from weakness, 'because the greatest of all have been in a good state of health'. Recalling the melancholy in earlier years, it was Sarah's experience that

> the strength of grace and divine light has wholly conquered these disadvantages and carried the mind, in a constant manner, quite above all such effects. Since the resignation spoken of before nearly three years ago (1740), everything of that nature seems to be overcome and crushed by the power of faith and trust in God, and resignation to Him ... This steadiness and constancy has remained through great outward changes

> and trials; such as times of the most extreme pain, and apparent hazard of immediate death (I.376b).

As to the fruit borne, Edwards marks a new and deeper spirit of worship, such that Sarah expressed 'a longing to sit and sing this life away' (I.377b). There were often vehement longings and faintings after more love to Christ, and greater conformity to Him; especially longing after these two things; to be more perfect in humility and adoration.' (I.378a) A further note is sounded; one which, given its essential gospel mandate, silences any and all critics: there was a great sense 'of the duty of charity to the poor, and how much the generality of Christians come short in the practice of it'.

For all that was done in and through Mrs Edwards, there was 'no appearance of spiritual pride; but on the contrary, with a very great increase of meekness and humility, and a disposition in honour to prefer others, as well as a great aversion to judging others' (I.lxviiib). This, as we shall see, is a clear and distinguishing mark of a true work of God. Mr Edwards brings these final words of assessment to bear:

> Now if these things are enthusiasm, and the fruits of a distempered brain, let my brain be evermore possessed of that happy distemper! If this be distraction, I pray God that the world of mankind may be all seized with this benign, meek, beneficent, beautiful, glorious distraction!

And what notions have they of religion, that reject what has been described, as not true religion! What shall we find to answer those expressions in Scripture: the peace of God that passes all understanding; rejoicing with joy unspeakable and full of glory, in believing in and loving an unseen Saviour; all joy and peace in believing; God's shining in our hearts, to give the light of the knowledge of the glory of God, in the face of Jesus Christ; with open face, beholding as in a mirror the glory of the Lord, and being changed into the same image, from glory to glory, even as by the Sprit of the Lord; having the love of God shed abroad in our hearts, by the Holy Spirit given to us – I say, if those things which have been mentioned, do not answer these expressions, what else can we find out that does?

Those that do not think such things as these be the fruits of the true Spirit, would do well to consider what kind of spirit they are waiting and praying for, and what sort of fruits they expect he should produce when He comes. I suppose it will generally be allowed, that there is such a thing as a glorious outpouring of the Spirit of God to be expected, to introduce very joyful and glorious times upon religious accounts; times wherein holy love and joy will be raised to a great height in true Christians; but, if those things be rejected, what is left that we can find wherewith to patch up a notion, or form an idea, of the high, blessed, joyful religion of these times? What is there sweet, excellent, and joyful, of a religious nature, that is entirely of a different nature from these things? (I.378b).

Having reviewed Jonathan and Sarah's personal experiences of the renewing work of the Spirit, we now turn to more theological reflections. Before we proceed, however, it must be understood that the key to understanding Edwards' writings, as with any author, is knowing the *reasons* he wrote. His first published book was titled: *A Faithful Narrative of the Surprising work of God in the Conversion of Many Hundred Souls in Northampton and the Neighbouring Towns and Villages of New Hampshire, in New England*, and was submitted 6 November, 1736, in answer to a request. The Rev. Dr Coleman of Boston had heard about the revival in Northampton, and asked Edwards for details. Coleman was so impressed with the brief account that Edwards sent him, he asked for a 'fuller statement'; this was forwarded to England, to two of Coleman's friends, the hymn writer, Dr Isaac Watts, and Dr John Guyse.

What characterizes this first work is its descriptive nature; of particular note is his documentation of unusual physical manifestations accompanying the renewal dynamics. In later writings, Edwards would reflect on things theologically, even philosophically, in an attempt to make the experiences and dynamics of revival understandable. But in his *Narrative,* he concentrates on the specific manifestations accompanying the 'remarkable revival of religion'. Start to finish, however, the focal concern in all his writings was the nature of true religion, and in that, the relation between the invisible action of the Spirit on the human heart, and the visible, bodily effects of His manifest presence.

Edwards' Northampton congregation – *before* the revival – has been described as 'respectable, good people, who possessed a kind of rote orthodoxy which shuffled doctrines aimlessly like faded packs of cards. Their concerns were not God and His Kingdom, but land and the pursuit of affluence.' A large part of the town's population attended the one church, but the majority of the membership had long since lost a vitality to their faith and commitments. The people continued to go through the motions of religion without partaking of its power and joy. Under Edwards' anointed leadership, the Holy Spirit opened hearts and illumined faith, such that 'their opaque orthodoxy suddenly became a transparent medium through which they saw the glory of God'.[5]

Northampton's worship, their witness, their whole way of life became *impassioned;* and theirs was the fire of God that spread, not only over most of New England, but to Britain and beyond. So much so that even secular historians speak of 'The Great Awakening'. With the re-convictions, conversions and spiritual transformations that issued from the Great Awakening, there were unfamiliar 'manifestations', the outward signs and demonstrations of the Spirit's immediate presence. Watts and Guyse write in their Preface to the *Narrative,*

[5] *The Great Awakening: Documents on the Revival of Religion, 1740–45,* edited by Richard Bushman, Atheneum, New York, 1970, p. 3.

> Never did we hear or read, since the first ages of Christianity, any event of this kind so surprising as the present Narrative hath set before us . . . . It pleased God, two years ago, to display His free and sovereign mercy in the conversion of a great multitude of souls in a short space of time, turning them from a formal, cold, and careless profession of Christianity, to the lively exercise of every Christian grace, and the powerful practice of our holy religion (I.344).

Again and again, Edwards writes of 'extraordinary affections', accompanied by physical demonstrations of fear, sorrow, love, joy; of 'tears, trembling, groans, loud outcries, agonies of the body, and the failing of bodily strength', of 'fits, jerks and convulsions'. He had done his research, stating, 'I have particularly conversed with persons, about their experiences, who belong to all parts of the country and in various parts of Connecticut, and have been informed of the experiences of many others by their own pastors' (I.359a).

The following sample from Edwards' writings helps put an historical background to the kinds of things experienced at the Airport Vineyard meetings; while the manifestations may be new to many of us, they are not untypical experiences when the Spirit of God comes to renew His people. Many who have been to the Airport meetings will find their personal experiences mirrored in the following accounts.

> In the latter part of December, the Spirit of God began extraordinarily to set in, and wonderfully to work amongst us; and there were, very suddenly, one after another, five or six persons, who were to all appearances savingly converted, and some of them wrought upon in a very remarkable manner (I.348a).

As to the public assemblies, the congregation was frequently in tears, 'some weeping with sorrow and distress, others with joy and love, others with pity and concern for neighbours'. Church members of long standing 'were greatly enlivened, and renewed with fresh and extraordinary [experiences] of the Spirit of God. Many who had laboured under difficulties about their own state [regarding their salvation], had now their doubts removed by more satisfying experiences, and more clear discoveries of God's love.' 'When this work first appeared, and was so extraordinarily carried on amongst us, others round about us seemed not to know what to make of it. Many scoffed at and ridiculed it; and some compared what we called conversion, to certain distempers' (I.348b).

Two parallels are of immediate note: the first, that timeless spirit of judgementalism and fault-finding seemed to have been as unfettered in Edwards' day as many currently experience it. Second, given the number of people who have come to the Airport Vineyard from considerable distance, and the 'transferability' that has been documented, the following citation is remarkable in its similarity:

> There were many instances of persons who came from abroad on visits, or on business, who had not been long here before . . . they were savingly wrought upon; and partook of that shower of blessing which God rained down here, and went home rejoicing, till at length the same work began evidently to appear to prevail in several other towns in the country (I.349a).

As he continues to describe the Northampton experience, Edwards offers these general comments on the work:

> God has also seemed to have gone out of His usual way, in the quickness of His work, and the swift progress His Spirit has made on the operations on the hearts of many. It is wonderful that persons should be so suddenly, and yet so greatly changed (I.350a).

As is stressed repeatedly at the Airport Vineyard, Edwards recognizes that God's work is unique in each individual, 'in the degrees both of awakening and conviction, and also of saving light, love and joy, that many have experienced . . . Some having been seized suddenly, others awakened gradually' (I.350b).

He has this very candid declaration, something which has been echoed repeatedly at the Airport Vineyard:

> It has been very observable, that persons of the greatest understanding, and who had studied most about things of this nature, have been more confounded than others.

> Some such persons declare, that all their former wisdom is brought to nought, and that they appear to have been mere babes who knew nothing (I.354b).

The pastor's heart beats strongly in the following citation, as Edwards reflects on the physical manifestations he has witnessed; his love for his people is boldly declared as he states:

> It was very wonderful to see how a person's affections were sometimes moved – when God did as it were suddenly open their eyes, and let into their minds a sense of the greatness of His grace, the fullness of Christ, and His readiness to save . . . Their joyful surprise has caused their hearts as it were to leap, so that they have been ready to break forth into laughter, tears often at the same time issuing like a flood, and intermingling a loud weeping. Sometimes they have not been able to forbear crying out with a loud voice, expressing their great admiration. In some, even the view of the glory of God's sovereignty, in the exercises of His grace, has surprised the soul with such sweetness, as to produce the same effects . . . (I.354b). The manner of God's work on the soul, sometimes especially, is very *mysterious* (I.355b).

By way of initial analysis, Edwards offers this as to the reasons his congregation experienced such extraordinary phenomena: 'They now have sight and taste of the divine excellency there is in the Gospel, which is more effectual to convince them, than reading many volumes or arguments without it.' 'They have *intuitively* beheld, and *immediately* felt, a most illustrious and powerful evidence of divinity in them.' As to his preaching, he says, 'The arguments are the same that they have heard hundreds of times; but the force of the arguments, and their conviction by them, is altogether new; they come with a new and before unexperienced power' (I.356a). 'Persons after their conversion often speak of religious things as seeming *new* to them: that preaching is a *new* thing; that it seems to them that they never heard preaching before; that the Bible is a *new* book: they find there *new* chapters, new psalms, *new* histories, because they see them in a new light.' 'Many have spoken much of their hearts being drawn out in love to God and Christ; and of their minds being wrapped up in delightful contemplation of the glory and wonderful grace of God . . .' (I.356b).

While Edwards made the previous generic assessments, he also made the following particular evaluations in respect of both grace and wisdom:

> There is a vast difference, as observed, in the *degree,* and also in the particular *manner* of a person's experiences . . . . [It is] evidently the *same* work, [and] it all tends to the same *end,* and it is plainly the *same Spirit* that breathes and acts in *various* persons. [But] there is endless *variety* in the particular manner and circumstances in which persons are wrought on; [by observation it can be concluded] that God is further

> from confining Himself to a particular method in His work on souls, than some imagine. I believe it has occasioned some good people amongst us, who were before, too ready to make their own experience a rule to others, to be less censorious and more *extended in their charity;* the work of God has been *glorious* in its variety; it has the more displayed the manifold and unsearchable wisdom of God, and wrought more charity among His people (I.357b).

A common misconception needs clarification here: without question, the move of God that characterized the Great Awakening brought thousands of the unsaved into the Kingdom; but the outpouring also had a radical effect on the church. As Tracy notes in his history of the Awakening, 'great numbers of church members were converted . . . . In some cases, the revival seems to have been almost wholly within the church, and to have resulted in the conversion of nearly all the members'.[6] Once the church was renewed and revived, mass evangelism was the *result.*

Having experienced what we've experienced at the Airport, this assessment of God's renewing, reviving work seems fitting, be it 257 years ago, or today:

> Certainly it becomes us, who profess the religion of

[6] Joseph Tracy, *The Great Awakening: A History,* New York Times, 1969, p. 391.

Christ, to take notice of ssuch astonishing exercises of His power and mercy, and give Him the glory which is due, when He begins to accomplish any of His promises concerning the latter days: and it gives us further encouragement to pray, and wait, and hope for the like display of His power in our midst. *The hand of the Lord is not shortened that it cannot save*, but we have reason to fear that our iniquities, our coldness in religion, and the general carnality of our spirits have raised a wall of separation between God and us . . . and seem to have provoked the Spirit of Christ to absent Himself much from our nation.

Return, O Lord, and visit Thy churches, and revive Thine own work in the midst of us.

From such blessed instances of the success of the Gospel as appear in this narrative, we may learn much of the way of the Spirit of God in His dealings with the souls of men, in order to convince sinners, and restore them to His favour and His image by Jesus Christ, His Son (I.344).

Not everyone, however, received news of the Awakening, and the unusual physical manifestations that accompanied the 'way of the Holy Spirit in His dealings with the souls of men' as graciously and as affirmingly as Watts and Guyse, the authors of the preceding quote. By 1742, opposition to the Awakening had long since ceased to be silent. Some were convinced that God was NOT working in the Awakening. Many believed the 'revival' was an emotional orgy that wantonly disturbed the churches and frustrated the true work of God.'[7] 'Enthusiasm' was the pejorative term used for religious fanaticism, an experiential spirituality in the extreme, unguided and unbridled by the Scriptures. In some circles, there was no acceptable connection between the convincing, convicting, renewing work of the Holy Spirit, and the reported bodily effects, the physical manifestations accompanying the revival.

Leading the opposition was a pastor from Boston, Charles Chauncy. He was the recognized spokesman for all New Englanders who resented or feared the emotions 'awakened' in the revival (p. 229). In a widely circulated document titled, *Overheated Passions, a Letter . . . to Mr. George Wishart, 1742,* Chauncy indicts Gilbert Tennent as an enthusiast for preaching in 'the extemporaneous Way, with much Noise and little Connection'.

Chauncy also accused the British evangelist George Whitefield, for under his ministry,

> the Multitudes, whose sensible Perceptions arose to such a Height, they cried out, fell down, swooned away, and, to all Appearance, were like persons in fits; the filling of the houses of worship with confusion is not to be expressed in words, nor indeed conceived of by the most lively imagination, unless where persons have been eye and ear witnesses to these things . . .

[7] Bushman, *op. cit.*, p.xiii.

In other words, seeing is believing, and even if you see it, you won't believe it.

> The shrieks they catch from one to another, till a great part of the congregation is affected . . . They move others, and bring forward a general scream. Visions now became common, and trances also. Subjects report that they have conversed with Christ and holy angels; had opened to them the book of Life, and were permitted to read the names of persons there, and the like. Laughing, loud hearty laughing, was one of the ways in which our new converts, almost everywhere, were wont to join together in expressing their joy and the conversion of others . . . at the same time, some would be praying, some exhorting, some singing, some clapping their hands, some laughing, some crying, some shrieking and roaring out . . . It is in the evening, or more late in the night, that there is the screaming and shrieking to the greatest degree. [8]

Several years after the initial outpouring of the Spirit, Edwards himself was questioning the depth of faith and sincerity of many newly 'revived'; this is more than reflected in his next published work, *The distinguishing marks of a work of the true Spirit with a particular consideration of the extraordinary circumstances with which this work is attended (November 1741).*

Again the work is prefaced by a 'senior minister', William Cooper. He writes,

[8] *Ibid.*, pp.118-19.

> The grace we are now under is certainly such as neither we nor our fathers have seen; and in some circumstances so wonderful, that I believe there has not been the like since the extraordinary pouring out of the Spirit immediately after our Lord's ascension. The apostolic times seem to have returned upon us: such a display has there been of the power and grace of the Spirit (2.258).

As he did in his *Narrative,* Edwards begins by describing what he has been seeing:

> By the providence of God, I have for some months past been much amongst those who have been the subjects of the work in question; and particularly, have been in the way of seeing and observing those extraordinary things with which many persons have been offended: such as persons' crying out aloud, shrieking, being put into great agonies of body, etc. – and have seen the manner and issue of such operations, and the fruits of them, for several months together; many of them being persons with whom I have been intimately acquainted (II.270a).

He then gives extended consideration to these manifestations, based on the text in 1 John 4:1: 'Beloved, believe not every spirit, but try the spirits whether they are of God; because many false prophets are gone out into the world.' Edwards begins:

> In the apostolic age, there was the greatest outpouring of the Spirit of God that ever was; both as to His extraordinary influences and gifts, and His ordinary operations, in convincing, converting, enlightening, and sanctifying the souls of men. But as the influences of the true Spirit abounded, so counterfeits did also abound; the devil was abundant in mimicking, both the ordinary and the extraordinary influences of the Spirit of God . . . This made it very necessary that the Church of Christ should be furnished with some certain rules [and] distinguishing marks. . . (II.260a).

He then asserts the following: we are to take the Scriptures as our guide, 'the great and standing rule which God has given to His Church, in order to guide them in things relating to the great concerns of their souls; and it is an infallible and sufficient rule' (II.260b).

Under that point, Edwards makes this essential distinction:

> What the *church* has been used to, is not a rule . . . because there may be new and extraordinary works of God [that He will yet bring] in an extraordinary manner. He has [previously] brought to pass new things, strange works; and has wrought in such a manner as to surprise both men and angels. The prophecies of Scripture give us reason to think that God has things to accomplish, which have never yet been seen. No deviation from what has [till now] been usual, let it be never so great, is an argument that a

> work is not from the Spirit of God, if it be no deviation from His prescribed rule . . . The Holy Spirit is sovereign in His operation; and we know that He uses a great variety; and we cannot tell how great a variety He may use, within the compass of the rules He Himself has fixed. We ought not to limit God where He has not limited Himself (II.261a).

At the meetings at the Airport Vineyard, counsel similar to Edwards' is given, but in a different form: John Arnott often reminds those gathered that there is no Scriptural basis for the common belief that 'the Holy Spirit is a gentleman, and does nothing without our consent.' Referring to the Apostle Paul's conversion experience, he asks, 'If someone in your church suddenly fell to the ground, heard his name called, and said that he had seen a vision, and was left blind after the whole experience, what would you conclude? And, how would you explain it to his mother?'

Edwards makes a most helpful distinction:

> [A work of the Spirit] is not to be judged of by any effects on the bodies of men; such as tears, trembling, groans, loud outcries, agonies of body, or the failing of bodily strength. The influence persons are under is not to be judged of one way or other by such effects on the body; and the reason is, because Scripture nowhere gives us any such rule.

Another of the pastors at the Airport Vineyard, Marc

Dupont, gives similar counsel, and brings to bear added insight. He makes it clear that we ought not to come seeking a particular manifestation – 'I want the joy . . .' – nor should we feel that God has 'passed us by' if nothing very dramatic seems to be happening physically. The issue is not the shaking, or falling, or laughter; rather, it is receiving the tailor-made gift that our Heavenly Father wants to impart to each of us as individuals, not so that we each are glorified in and of ourselves, but that the Body of Christ is built up and edified collectively.

Both Edwards and the pastors at the Airport do not take exception to the manifestations; what they are saying is 'Draw no conclusions, based *only* on the manifestations, either way, pro or con'. However, they readily recognize that:

> The misery of hell is doubtless so dreadful, and eternity so vast, that if a person should have a clear apprehension of that misery as it is, it would be more than this feeble frame could bear . . . A true sense of the glorious excellency of the Lord Jesus Christ, and of His wonderful dying love, and the exercise of a truly spiritual love and joy, should be such as to overcome bodily strength. We are all ready to own that no man can see God and live . . . therefore it is not at all strange that God should sometimes give His saints such foretastes of heaven, as to diminish their bodily strength . . . . When the thoughts are so fixed [on the glory of God] and the affections so strong – and the whole soul so engaged, ravished, and swallowed up, all other parts

> of the body are so affected, as to be deprived of their strength, and the whole frame ready to dissolve (II.261b and 263a).

Directly addressing the anti-enthusiasts and their concern over the furore that had been evidenced, Edwards asserts:

> When Christ's Kingdom came, by that remarkable pouring out of the Spirit in the apostles' days, it occasioned a great stir everywhere. What a mighty opposition was there in Jerusalem, on occasion of the great effusion of the Spirit! The affair filled the world with noise, and gave occasion to some to say of the apostles, that they had turned the world upside down (Acts 17:6; II.262b).

There were some who took exception to the 'new' practice of testimonial, of people publicly describing their personal experiences. Edwards answers, 'Scripture is full of examples of one person being influenced by the good example of another. (Matthew 5:16; 1 Peter 3:1; 1 Timothy 4:12; Titus 2:7; 2 Corinthians 8:1-7; Hebrews 4:12; Philippians 3:17). There never yet was a time of remarkable pouring out of the Spirit, and great revival of religion, but that example had a main hand'(II.263b). While advocating the importance of testimony, Edwards did recognize that it would be some time before we saw 'pure God' in one another. For that reason, it neither surprised nor dissuaded him when he saw 'imprudences and irregularities of conduct'.

> The end for which God pours out His Spirit is to make men holy, and not to make them politicians. It is no wonder that in a mixed multitude of all sorts – wise and unwise, young and old, weak and strong natural abilities, under strong impressions of mind – there are many who behave themselves imprudently . . . A thousand imprudences will not prove a work not to be of the Spirit of God . . .
>
> [Excess] may thus be accounted for from the remaining darkness and corruption of those that are yet the subjects of the saving influences of God's Spirit and have a real zeal for God.

In other words, 'God isn't finished with any one of us yet'.

By way of a biblical precedent, Edwards cites the New Testament Church of Corinth,

> a people who partook largely of that great effusion of the Spirit in the apostles' days, among whom there nevertheless abounded imprudences and great irregularities. There is scarcely any church more celebrated in the New Testament for being blessed with large measures of the Spirit of God, yet what manifold imprudences, great and sinful irregularities, and strange confusions (II.264b).

With grace, patience and biblical 'long-suffering', he counsels,

> When daylight first appears after a night of darkness, we must expect to have darkness mixed with light for

a while, and not have perfect day and the sun risen at once. The fruits of the earth are first green before they are ripe, and come to their proper perfection gradually; and so, Christ tells us, is the Kingdom of God (Mark 4.26-28; II.271a).

With similar grace, John Arnott frequently asks the congregation for permission to correct any of those whose behaviour seems excessive or inappropriate; John then asks that the congregation be forgiving, if, in the concern for 'decency and order', they overstep themselves, and correct what was legitimately Spirit-inspired.

It is not only fleshly excess, however, that brings distortion and compromise within the renewing work of the Spirit. There is introduced a further note, one which will receive greater attention in subsequent writings. In *Distinguishing Marks*, there is this added observation regarding errors in conduct: 'Satan will keep men secure as long as he can; but when he can do that no longer, he often endeavours to drive them to extremes, and so to dishonour God, and wound religion in that way' (II.271b).

With this groundwork laid, Edwards presses on to ask, 'What ARE distinguishing marks of a true work of the Spirit of God?'

Front and centre, he asserts, 'If the spirit that is at work among a people is plainly observed to work so as to convince them of Christ, and lead them to Him . . . it is a sure sign that it is the true and right Spirit' (II.266b). Second, are there signs that the interests of Satan's kingdom are being assaulted? 'Are persons drawn off from the world and weaned from the objects of their worldly lusts, and taken off from worldly pursuits, by the sense they have of the excellency of divine things, and the affections they have to spiritual enjoyments?' (II.267b).

Third, is there evidence of a greater regard to the Scriptures, establishing believers more and more in truth and godliness? The devil certainly isn't going to have us fall in love with the Word. 'Would the prince of darkness, in order to promote his kingdom of darkness, lead men to the sun? . . . He hates every word of the Bible, and we may be sure that he never will attempt to raise a person's esteem of affection to it' (II.267b).

Fourth, is there a greater spirit of love to God and man? Citing 1 John 4:12–13, Edwards takes Christian faith back to basics:

> This last mark which the apostle gives of the true Spirit he seems to speak of as the most eminent: love to God and men . . . The surest character of true divine supernatural love – distinguishing it from counterfeits that arise from a natural self-love – is that the Christian virtue of humility shines in it; that which above all others renounces, abases, and annihilates what we term self. Christian love or true charity is a humble love (II.268b).

Recognizing excess, spiritual immaturity, and fleshly

exuberance for what it is, Edwards offers the following 'no-nonsense' counsel by way of discernment of spirits:

> These things the devil *would not do* if he could: awaken the conscience and make men sensible of their miserable state by reason of their sin, and sensible of their great need of a Saviour; and he would not confirm men in their belief that Jesus is the Son of God, and the Saviour of sinners; he would not beget in men's minds... the truth of the Holy Scriptures, or incline them to make use of them; nor would he show men the truth, in things that concern their soul's interest; to undeceive them, and lead them out of darkness into light, and give them a view of things as they really are. The devil *neither can nor will* give men a spirit of divine love, or Christian humility and poverty of spirit . . . these things are as contrary as possible to his nature. Therefore, when there is an extraordinary influence or operation appearing on the minds of people, if these things are found in it, we are safe in determining that it is the work of God, whatever other circumstances it may be attended with, whatever instruments are used, and whatever methods are taken to promote it; whatever means a sovereign God, whose judgements are [very] deep, employs to carry it on; whatever effects may be wrought on men's bodies . . . They plainly show *the finger of God,* and are sufficient to outweigh a thousand such little objections, as many make from oddities, irregularities, errors in conduct, and the

delusions and scandals of some professors (II.269a).

Even after such instruction, many still felt unsettled by the manifestations accompanying the Great Awakening. And so the accusation was rendered, 'God cannot be the author of it, because He is the God of order, not of confusion'. This is an indictment that is brought repeatedly against the Airport meetings. Regrettably, those bringing forward the accusation rarely stay around long enough to interview those who are the subjects of the unsettling behaviour, and in so doing, are drawing conclusions prematurely.

In answering that things were not being done 'decently and in order', Edwards contrasts the upsetting of a worship service with the renewal and transformation of a life. He says, 'The conviction of sinners for their conversion is the end of religious means' (II.271a). Consider a gospel example: the *end* of the deliverance of the Gadarene demoniac was a new decency and order – the man formally named 'Legion' sat at the Lord's feet, clothed and in his right mind; the *means* to that deliverance was noisy, unruly, and even riotous, especially if the stampede of pigs is included! (Luke 8:26-39). Edwards comments,

> If God is pleased to convince the consciences of persons, so that they cannot avoid great outward manifestations, even to interrupting and breaking off those public means they were attending, I do not think this is confusion, or an unhappy interruption, any more

> than if a company should meet on the field to pray for rain, and should be broken off from their exercise by a plentiful shower.

With almost unguarded abandon, he continues:

> Would to God that all the public assemblies in the land were broken off from their exercise with such confusion as this the next sabbath day! We need not be sorry for breaking the order of means, by obtaining the end to which that order is directed. He that is going to fetch a treasure, need not be sorry that he is stopped, by meeting the treasure in the midst of his journey (II.271a).

As discerning, wise and prolific as Edwards was, many were still unconvinced. In speaking to those who were playing 'watch and see', those who distanced themselves from the renewing, reviving work of God in their midst, Edwards writes:

> I would entreat those who quiet themselves, that they proceed on a principle of prudence, and are waiting to see the issue of things, and what fruits those that are the subjects of this work will bring forth in their lives – to consider whether this will justify a long refraining from acknowledging Christ when He appears so wonderfully and graciously present in the land.
>
> It is probable that many of those who are thus waiting, know not for *what* they are waiting. If they

> wait to see a work of God *without* difficulties and stumbling blocks, it will be like the fool's waiting at the river side to have the water all run by.
>
> A work of God without stumbling blocks is never to be expected. 'It must needs be that offences come.' There never yet was any great manifestation that God made of Himself to the world, without many difficulties attending to it. . . This pretended prudence, in persons waiting so long before they acknowledge this work, will probably in the end prove the greatest imprudence. Hereby they will fail of any share of so great a blessing, and will miss the most precious opportunity of obtaining divine light, grace, and comfort, heavenly and eternal benefits that God ever gave in New England. While the glorious fountain is set open in so wonderful a manner, and multitudes flock to it and receive a rich supply for the want of their souls, they stand at a distance, doubting, wondering, and receiving nothing, and are like to continue thus till the precious season is past (II.273a).

He cites Acts 5:38-9, and Gamaliel's counsel: 'If this . . . be of human origin, it will collapse; but if it be of God . . . you risk finding yourself at war with God.' Edwards then says:

> There is no kind of sin so hurtful and dangerous to the souls of men, as those committed against the Holy Ghost and His gracious operations on the hearts of men. Nothing will so much tend forever to prevent our

> having any benefit of His operations on our own souls (II.273b).

He concludes with these words:

> Since the great God has come down from heaven, and manifested Himself in so wonderful a manner in this land, it is vain for any of us to expect any other than to be greatly affected by it in our spiritual state and circumstances, respecting the favour of God, one way or another. Those who do not become more happy by it, will become far more guilty and miserable . . . . To friends of this work, who have been partakers of it, and are zealous to promote it . . . humility and self-diffidence and an entire dependence of our Lord Jesus Christ will be our best defence. Let us therefore maintain the strictest watch against spiritual pride, or being lifted up with extraordinary experiences and comforts, and the high favours of heaven, that any of us may have received . . . When we have great discoveries of God made to our souls, we should not shine bright in our own eyes (II.273b - II.274a).

Charles Chauncy read Edwards' *Distinguishing Marks,* and he too, studied and observed the unusual phenomena the revival generated. He responded, putting together a 'compendium of horror stories' about the worst extravagances of the Awakening. Chauncy solicited the material from correspondents throughout New England, collecting eyewitness accounts wherever he could. He titled his work, *Enthusiasm Described and Caution'd Against, (1742)*.

Chauncy defined the enthusiast as one 'who has a conceit of himself as a person favoured with the extraordinary presence of the deity. He mistakes the workings of his own passions for divine communications, and fancies himself immediately inspired by the Spirit of God, when all the while, he is under no other influence than that of an over-heated imagination.'[9] Chauncy is concerned with private, personal experience that supersedes biblical revelation. Immovably cessationist, he asserts:

> The work of the Spirit is different now from what it was in the first days of Christianity. Men were then favoured with the extraordinary presence of the Spirit. He came upon them in miraculous gifts and powers; as a spirit of prophecy, or knowledge, or revelation, of tongues, of miracles; *but the Spirit is not now to be expected in these ways.* His grand business lies in preparing men's minds for the grace of God, by true humiliation, from an apprehension of sin, and the necessity of a Saviour; then in working in them faith and repentance, and such a change as shall turn them from the power of sin and satan unto God; and in fine, by carrying on the good work He has begun in them; assisting them in duty, strengthening them against

[9] *Ibid.*, p. 291 and p. 231.

temptation, and in a word, preserving them blameless through faith unto salvation. And all this He does by the Word and prayer, as the great means in the accomplishment of these purposes of mercy.

> Herein, in general, consists the work of the Spirit. It does not lie in giving men private revelations, but in opening their minds to understand the public ones contained in the Scripture. It does not lie in sudden impulses and impressions, or in immediate calls and extraordinary missions.[10]

With anti-revolutionary zeal, Chauncy's operative theology of 'Father, Son and Holy Book' is declared in bold relief:

> You cannot, my brethren, be too well acquainted with what the Bible makes the work of the Holy Ghost, in the affair of salvation: And if you have upon your minds a clear and distinct understanding of this, it will be a powerful guard to you against all enthusiastical impressions . . . This adherence to the Bible, my brethren, is one of the best preservatives against enthusiasm. If you will but express a due reverence to this Book of God, making it the great rule of judgement, even in respect of the Spirit's influences and operations, you will not be in much danger of being led into delusion. Let this be your inquiry under all supposed impulses from the Spirit, 'What saith the

[10] *Ibid.*, p. 244, emphasis added.

> Scripture?' If your impressions, and imagined spiritual motions agree not therewith, 'tis because there is no hand of the Spirit of God in them: They are only the workings of your own imaginations, or something worse; and must at once, without any more ado, be rejected as such.[11]

He concludes his instruction with this myopic assertion: 'Let us fetch our notions of religion from the Scripture.'[12] One wonders what Chauncy would have written in response to the outline of a biblical foundation for the experiences of the manifest presence of God that constitute Chapter 3 of this work!

What we do have is Edwards' responses to many of Chauncy's indictments, addressed in his longest work to date, *Thoughts Concerning the Present Revival in New England and the way in which it ought to be acknowledged and promoted (1742).*

In it, however, Chauncy and the anti-enthusiasts are no longer centre-stage when it comes to Edwards' concerns.

Over the years, the number and frequency of 'imprudences' had increased, and fanaticism needed to be checked. In the summer of 1741, the Rev. James Davenport was dubiously credited with igniting spiritual wild fire that began to burn out of control. Winslow records this report:

[11] *Ibid.*, p. 246. It is of note that later in his life, Chauncy gave leadership to the Unitarians. See William DeArteaga's *Quenching the Spirit*, Creation House, Altamonte, Florida, 1992, p. 53.
[12] *Ibid.*, p. 254.

> It was not long before indecorum outdid itself under the notion that the greater the clamour the more the Spirit of God was at work. Zeal was more important than knowledge. An exhorter who could boast of no education was thought better qualified to arouse sinners than the minister. A premium was likewise placed on youth and inexperience. A blind boy memorized Whitefield's sermons, spoke them with violent gestures, and was thought a great preacher.[13]

Here both Edwards and Chauncy shared similar concerns: both were concerned with separating the 'wheat from the chaff'. The contrast lay in their focus – Edwards fixed his attention on the wheat, while Chauncy concentrated on the chaff. It is interesting to note that it was Edwards, not Chauncy, who pleaded for the finer and more careful sifting, a more discriminating discernment.

As chief spokesman for the Awakening; it was as if Edwards found himself riding a bicycle, and he is painfully aware that he could fall off on either side. He attempts to maintain a balanced position, by dedicating himself to travel the critical equilibrium maintaining both reason and emotion, while avoiding the extremes of unfeeling, speculative rationalism on the one hand, and unchecked, anti-intellectual 'enthusiasm' on the other. So, Edwards writes to both the Awakening's greatest detractors, and its best friends.

[13] Ola Elizabeth Winslow, *Jonathan Edwards, A Biography.* Macmillan Company, New York, 1940, p.198.

In *Thoughts,* he debates the validity of the revival against these two fronts: on one side, a decided opposition to the emotional and physical manifestations; on the other, those who saw no dangers whatsoever, those who proceeded without any cautions, checks or balances. As has been documented, Edwards had long recognized excess for what it is, and made due allowance for it. Many are familiar with the title of Edwards' most famous sermon, 'Sinners in the Hands of an Angry God'. That particular sermon was preached at least two other times; it achieved notoriety *only* when he preached it at the height of all the revival excitement in Enfield, Connecticut. Things had been 'running wild', some pretty goofy things taking place. One commented, 'Its effectiveness owed much to the frenzied moment.' Another, 'He preached into chaos itself, the Great Awakening having been dubbed, *The Great Clamour*.'[14] Another biographer explained: 'In the atmosphere of barely controlled hysteria that pervaded, the bleak rhetoric proved terrifying.'[15] It is understatement to say that Edwards' sermon came as a sobering counterpoint.

The work, *Thoughts Concerning the Present Revival,* further reflects Edwards' primary concerns. The longest section of the five main divisions of the book gives indication as to where Edwards saw the greatest problem: *Part IV, Showing what things are to be corrected or avoided in promoting the work, or in our behaviour under it.* This section is directed to the enthusiastic friends of the revival; the

[14] *Ibid.*, p. 190; also, Winslow, *Jonathan Edwards, Basic Writings,* Meridian, New York, 1966, p.150.

[15] Patricia Tracy, *Jonathan Edwards, Pastor,* Hill and Wang, N.Y. 1979.

concern is pushed to the forefront: 'One truly zealous person, in the time of such an event, that seems to have a great hand in the affair, and draws the eyes of many upon him, may do more harm to hinder the work, than a hundred great, and strong, and open opposers' (I.398a). As Edwards saw it, the future of the revival depended on whether or not wild fire and fanaticism could be contained and corrected.[16]

Very much aware of the truth of Edwards' insights here, the pastors at the Airport Vineyard continue to try to manage 'wild fire' as it breaks out. While welcoming the Spirit's transformative work, the more exuberant manifestations are neither highlighted nor trophied; rather, the question is asked repeatedly: 'Tell us more about your relationship with Jesus.'

In *Thoughts,* Edwards recognizes an unseen warfare working against the revival. While he but mentions the work of Satan in his previous writings, Edwards has come to see evidence of a greater malice at work. The quote in the paragraph above has this sentence preceding it: 'Though the devil will [be] diligent in stirring up the open enemies of religion, he yet [employs another strategy], for in a time of revival of religion, his main strength shall be tried with the friends of it; and he will chiefly exert himself in his attempts to mislead them' (I.398a).

Despite the abuses and excesses, Edwards is still unashamed and unabashed to describe, favourably, the

[16] Iain Murray, *Jonathan Edwards, a New Biography,* Banner of Truth Trust, Edinburgh, 1992, p.238.

manifestations he has witnessed. He again documents what he has witnessed:

> There has, before now, been both crying out and falling . . . There have been many instances, before now, of persons in this town fainting with joyful discoveries made to their souls, and once several together. And there have been several instances here of persons waxing cold and benumbed, with their hands clenched, yea, and their bodies in convulsions, being overpowered with a strong sense of the astonishing great and excellent things of God and the eternal world (I.370b).

It should be recalled that it is in *Thoughts* that Edwards uses his wife's extended testimony as a model and example of spiritual integrity, concluding, 'Now if these things are enthusiasm, and the fruits of a distempered brain, let my brain be evermore possessed of that happy distemper!' (I.378b).

In addressing Chauncy and the anti-enthusiasts, Edwards begins with a call to humility in faith. He counsels that if we judge too quickly, we may well be rebuked for our arrogance. He grounds his counsel on Isaiah 40:13–14, 'Who has directed the Spirit of the Lord, or being His counsellor has taught Him?' John 3:8, 'The wind blows where it will and you hear the sound of it, but you do not know where it comes from or where it is going,' and Isaiah 2:17, 'Pride will be brought low and loftiness humbled, and the Lord alone will be exalted,'

Responding to Chauncy's 'adherence to the Bible' admonition, Edwards says,

> If we take the Scriptures for our rule, then the greater and higher [will be] our exercise of love to God, delight and complacency in Him, desires and longings after Him, delight in His children, love to mankind, brokenness of heart, abhorrence of sin, and self-abhorrence for it; the more we have of the peace of God which passes understanding, and joy in the Holy Ghost, unspeakable and full of glory, the higher our admiring thoughts of God, exulting and glorifying in Him . . . raised in the soul.
>
> It is a stumbling block to some, that religious affections should seem to be so powerful, or that they should be so violent, in some persons. They are therefore ready to doubt whether it can be the Spirit of God; or, whether this vehemence be not rather a sign of the operation of an evil spirit. But why should such a doubt arise? What is represented in Scripture as more powerful in its effects than the Spirit of God?[17] (I.367b).

As though countering Chauncy's criticisms regarding 'enthusiastical impressions', Edwards brings these insights to bear on the inseparable connection between the revelation and renewal:

[17] Edwards refes to the following texts on the 'power of God:' Luke 1:35; 1 Corinthians 2:4; Ephesians 1:19, 3:7; Colossians 1:11; 2 Thessalonians 1:11, 2 Timothy 1:7, and states: 'So the Spirit is represented by a mighty wind and by fire, things most powerful in their operation' (I.368a).

> However kind to human nature the influences of the Spirit of God are, yet nobody doubts but that divine and eternal things, as they may be discovered, would overpower the nature of man in its present weak state; and that therefore the body, in its present weakness, is not fitted for the views, and pleasures, and employments of heaven. Were God to disclose but a little of that which is seen by saints and angels in heaven, our frail natures would sink under it. Let us rationally consider wrath, divine glory, the infinite love and grace in Jesus Christ, and the infinite importance of eternal things; and then how reasonable it is to suppose, that if God a little withdraw the veil, to let light into the soul – and give a view of the great things of another world in their transcendent and infinite greatness – that human nature, which is as the grass, a shaking leaf, a weak withering flower, should totter under such a discovery! Such a bubble is too weak to bear a weight so vast. Alas! No wonder therefore it is said, No man can see God and live (I.368b).

It can be conjectured that Edwards continues to address directly Chauncy's indictments; recall the latter's insistence, 'Let us fetch our notions of religion from the Scripture'. By way of biblical precedence for the physical phenomena witnessed, Edwards works from Habakkuk 3:16: 'When I heard, my belly trembled, my lips quivered at the voice, rottenness entered my bones, I trembled in myself, that I might rest in the day of trouble.' Edwards comments:

> This is an effect similar to what the discovery of the same majesty and wrath has had upon many in these days; and to the same purpose, to give them rest in the day of trouble, and save them from that wrath. The Psalmist also speaks of such an effect as *I* have often seen on persons under religious affections of late.[18]

Citing Malachi 3:10 he states:

> God is pleased sometimes, in dealing forth spiritual blessings to His people, in some respects to exceed the capacity of the vessel in its present scantiness; so that He not only fills it, but makes their cup to run over (Psalm 23:5) and pours out a blessing, sometimes, in such manner and measure that there is not room enough to receive it (I.368b).

Commenting on yet another of the manifestations, Edwards reflects on some of the more emotional outbursts: 'The spirit of those who have been in distress for the souls of others, so far as I can discern, seems not to be different from that of the apostle, who travailed for souls . . .' (Galatians 4:19) (I.369b).

> By way of some conclusions, Edwards draws the following: If God gives a great increase of discoveries of Himself, and of love to Him, the benefit is infinitely greater than the calamity . . . It is a great fault in us to limit a sovereign all-wise God, whose judgements are a great deep, and His ways past finding out, where He

[18] Emphasis added.

> has not limited Himself, and in things concerning which He has not told us what His ways shall be (I.369a).

Having encouraged a greater humility with respect to embracing the ways in which God brings revival, Edwards calls forth a greater graciousness in our conduct towards one another. The following counsel ought to cause us each to examine our own hearts:

> Censuring others is the worst disease with which this affair has been attended (I.373a). Critics pass judgement, and make their own experience the rule, and reject such things as are now professed and experienced, because they themselves never felt them . . . Have they not condemned such vehement affections, such high transports of love and joy, such pity and distress for the souls of others, and exercises of the mind that have such great effects, merely, or chiefly, because they knew nothing about them by experience? Persons are very ready to be suspicious of what they have not felt themselves . . .

With penetrating insight, he continues:

> We should distinguish the good from the bad, and not judge of the whole by the part . . . . When any profess to have received light and comforts from heaven, and to have had sensible communion with God, many are ready to expect that now they appear like angels, and

> not still like poor, feeble, blind, and sinful worms of the dust. There being so much corruption left in the hearts of God's own children, and its prevailing as it sometimes does, is indeed a mysterious thing, and always was a stumbling-block to the world (I.371a).

His conclusion to the issue articulates the razor's edge between judgementalism and true gospel discernment:

> What great allowances would we need that others should make for us? Perhaps much greater than we are willing to make for others. The great weakness of the greater part of mankind, in any affair that is new and uncommon, appears in not distinguishing, but either approving or condemning all in the lump (I.371b).

The criticisms brought against the Awakening now dealt with, Edwards next turns his attention to the 'friends' of the revival. 'The weakness of human nature has always appeared in times of great revival of religion, by a disposition to run to extremes, and get into confusion; and especially in these three things, enthusiasm, superstition, and intemperate zeal' (I.372b). On the forefront is the concern that unchecked enthusiasm and zeal feed 'unenlightened' religion that is in turn the breeding ground for fleshly excess. The issue is the *source* of affective religious experience. Religious enthusiasm shifts the centre from the true and gracious reviving work of the Spirit, and becomes preoccupied with human experience.

Even more damaging – both to the individual's personal faith, and the well-being of the community – is the tendency towards religious pride. Through the inordinate amount of attention given to personal experiences, the subtle and not so subtle exultation of the ego can mutate, and the 'self' can quickly rise to occupy position at centre.

For all that Chauncy brought against the Awakening, this was one of his most legitimate concerns:

> I can't see that men have been made better, if hereby be meant, their being formed to a nearer resemblance to the divine being in moral holiness. 'Tis not evident to me, that persons, generally, have a better understanding of religion, a better government of their passions, a more Christian love to their neighbour, or that they are more decent and regular in their devotions towards God . . .
>
> What is a grand discriminating mark of this work, is that it makes men spiritually proud and conceited and uncharitable, to neighbours, to relations, even the nearest and dearest; to ministers in an especial manner; yea, to all mankind, who are not as they are, and don't think and act as they do.[19]

Edwards more than shared similar concerns; he titles the first section of Part IV, *One cause of errors attending a great revival of religion is undiscerned spiritual pride.* He states unequivocally:

[19] Bushman, *op. cit.*, p. 120.

> The first and the worst cause of errors, that prevail in such a state of things, is *spiritual pride.* This is the main door by which the devil comes into the hearts of those who are zealous for the advancement of religion. This is the main handle by which the devil has hold of religious persons, and the chief source of all the mischief that he introduces, to clog and hinder a work of God. This cause is the main spring, or at least the main support, of all the rest . . . I know that a great many things at this day are very injuriously laid to the pride of those that are zealous in the cause of God (I.399a).

With even greater forthrightness than Chauncy, Edwards marks the problem:

> It has been the manner in some places, or at least the manner of some persons, to speak of almost everything that they see amiss in others, in the most harsh, severe, and terrible language. It is frequent with them to say of others' opinions, or conduct, or advice – or of their coldness, their silence, their caution, their moderation, their prudence, etc. – that they are from the devil, or from hell; that such a thing is devilish, or hellish or cursed.

With the issue named in graphic terms, Edwards analyses the source:

> Spiritual pride is upon many accounts the most hateful,

> it is most like the devil; most like the sin he committed in a heaven of light and glory, where he was exalted high in divine knowledge, honour, beauty, and happiness. Pride is much more difficult to be discerned than any other corruption, because its nature very much consists in a person's having too high a thought of himself.

What follows is a circular argument: the sense that one is 'right' precludes evaluation and correction. If there was any doubt, there would be no grounds for certainty. 'Those that are spiritually proud, have a high conceit of these two things, their light, and their humility; both of which are a strong prejudice against a discovery of their pride' (I.399b).

The monks of old put it more simply: 'When a proud man thinks he is humble, his case is hopeless.' The corrective shines like a beacon: 'Nothing sets a person so much out of the devil's reach as humility, and so prepares the mind for true divine light without darkness, and so clears the eye to look on things as they truly are' (I.399a). Edwards is uncompromising in his counsel:

> God's own people should be the more jealous of themselves with respect to [pride] at this day, because the temptations that many have to this sin are exceedingly great . . . We had need therefore to have the greatest watch imaginable over our hearts . . . and to cry most earnestly to the great searcher of hearts for His help. He that trusts his own heart is a fool (I.399b).

Spiritual pride was not Edwards' only cause for concern, for he saw a larger source to religious excess. He addresses what he considers a further error that attends a great revival of religion: an ignorance of 'Satan's advantages and devices' (I.398b). 'When the devil . . . finds he can keep men quiet and secure no longer, then he drives them to excesses and extravagances. He holds them back as long as he can; but when he can do it no longer, then he will push them on, and, if possible, run them upon their heads' (I.397b). Fully cognizant of the bi-polar reactions and extremes evidenced in the Awakening, Edwards writes,

> The devil has driven the pendulum far beyond its proper point of rest; and when he has carried it to the utmost length that he can, and it begins by its own weight to swing back, he probably will set in, and drive it with the utmost fury the other way; and so give us no rest; and if possible prevent our settling in a proper medium (I.420b).

With true resurrection confidence, Edwards settles fearful concerns regarding deception: 'Though the devil be strong, yet, in such a war as this, he depends more on his craft than his strength' (I.390b). This is, in effect, what pastor John Arnott and others continually counsel at the Airport Vineyard: 'God's desire to bless us is far greater than Satan's ability to deceive us.' It is far healthier to focus attention on the wheat, and not the chaff, nor on the enemy sowing weeds. (Matthew 13:24-30) And so Edwards writes:

> The divine power of this work has marvellously appeared in some instances I have been acquainted with; in supporting and fortifying the heart under great trials . . . and in wonderfully maintaining the serenity, calmness, and joy of the soul, in an immovable rest in God, and sweet resignation to Him. And some under the blessed influences of this work have, in a calm, bright, joyful frame of mind, been carried through the valley of the shadow of death. Is it not strange that in a Christian country, and such a land of light as this is, there are many at a loss to conclude whose work this is, whether the work of God or the work of the devil? Is it not a shame to New England that such a work should be much doubted here? (I.375b).

With clear focus on the 'wheat', the following stands as summary to *Thoughts Concerning the Present Revival:*

> Whatever imprudences there have been, and whatever sinful irregularities; whatever vehemence of the passions, and heats of the imagination, transports, and ecstasies: whatever error in judgement, and indiscreet zeal; and whatever outcries, faintings, and agitations of body; yet, it is manifest and notorious, that there has been of late a very uncommon influence upon the minds of a very great part of the inhabitants of New England, attended with the best effects (I.374a).

Edwards continued to reflect upon and evaluate the fruit

borne of the revival. Nine years after the first outpouring, he produced *The Revival of Religion in Northampton, 1740-1742*, a letter Edwards wrote on 12 December, 1743, to a friend of the Awakening, a pastor in Boston. In it, he gives an account not only of the years named in the head he gives the letter, 1740-1742, but also the initial years 1734-1735, for they were both prelude to the Awakening of 1740-1742 and one of its major causes. Edwards' first account of the revival, published in 1736, alerted both Old England and New to the possibility and process of remarkable conversion, and the experience of the power and joy Christian faith offered.

Several things stand out in this later critical reflection. Of particular note is his frequent observation that the revival first, and often primarily, touched the 'professors' – not the academics in town, but Edwards' term for those who already 'professed' Christ – Christians – in other words. Conversions were certainly noted, and rejoiced in; but the balance of the Awakening came to those already established in faith. This is certainly the case at the meetings that the Vineyard is hosting; by far, the vast majority of those who have experienced something of renewal would be, in Edwards' terms, 'professors'; though a significant number, first-time conversions represent a very small percentage of those who have come under the Spirit's reviving influence. An example that Edwards cites, in an equivalent of a kinship or small house group meeting, is one which directly parallels the experience of thousands of believers at the Airport meetings:

> Several professors were so greatly affected with a sense of the greatness and glory of divine things, and the infinite importance of the things of eternity, that they were not able to conceal it – the affection of their minds overcoming their strength, and having a very sensible effect on their bodies . . . The affection was quickly propagated throughout the room; many appeared to be overcome with a sense of the greatness and glory of divine things, and with admiration, love, joy, and praise, and compassion to others . . . and many others at the same time were overcome with distress, about their sinful and miserable condition; so that the whole room was full of nothing but outcries, faintings and the like. It continued thus for some hours (I.lviiia).

Another significant aspect is illustrated in this work: Edwards still is unashamed of the manifestations. As is evident by now, in Edwards' writings we have the restrained prose of his time and culture; it is not *Wayne's World*, 'totally awesome party dudes!' Nevertheless, he writes that with the

> great revivings, quickenings, and comforts of professors, and the extraordinary external effects of these things, it was a very frequent thing to see outcries, faintings, convulsions, and such like, both with distress, and also admiration and joy. It was not the manner here to hold meetings all night, nor was it common to continue them till very late in the night; *but it was pretty often so,* that there were some so

> affected, and their bodies so overcome, that they could not go home, but were obliged to stay all night where they were (I.lviiib).

Again, writing predominantly of the experience of the 'professors', 'many, who had been formerly wrought upon, and in the time of our declension had fallen away into decays . . . now passed under a very remarkable new work of the Spirit of God, as if they had been the subjects of a second conversion' (I.lixa). Further,

> many have had their religious affections raised far beyond what they had ever been before: and there were some instances of persons lying in a sort of trance, remaining perhaps for a whole twenty-four hours motionless, and with their senses locked up; but in the meantime under strong imaginations, as though they went to heaven and had there a vision of glorious and delightful objects. But when the people were raised to this height, Satan took the advantage, and his interposition soon became apparent in many instances; and a great deal of caution and pains were found necessary to keep the people, many of them from running wild (I.lixb).

In considering the ebb and flow of 'liveliness of affections in religion', Edwards marks some of the fruit that has been recognized in the interim times – among them he names a sense of the nearness of God, and the enjoyment of 'many of the sensible tokens and fruits of His gracious presence' (I.lxia). He very insightfully critiques an issue that is repeatedly brought forward as a question: because the outward manifestations are so demonstrative, what of those who manifest very little, who don't fall down, or shake, or roll around with uncontrollable laughter, or whatever? Edwards categorically declares:

> the degree of grace is by no means to be judged of by the degree of *joy,* or the degree of *zeal;* and that indeed we cannot at all determine by these things, who are gracious and who are not; and that it is not the degree of religious affections, but the nature of them, that is chiefly to be looked at. Some that have had very great raptures of joy, and have been extraordinarily *filled* (as the vulgar phrase is,) and have had their bodies overcome, and that very often, have manifested far less of the [character] of Christians in the conduct since, than some others that have been still, and have made no great outward show. But then again, there are *many others* that have had extraordinary joys and emotions of mind, with frequent great effects upon their bodies, that behave themselves steadfastly, as humble, amiable, eminent Christians (I.lxib).

To the Scriptural mandate, 'by their fruit you shall know them', Edwards adds, 'by their *roots . . .*' Unless rooted in God's grace in Christ, so-called fruit, as impressive as they may be – spiritual visions, ecstasies, revelations or any manner of physical manifestation – they are deception and lie. Fruit presuppose roots.

It was this conviction that called forth *A Treatise Concerning Religious Affections.* Edwards preached the substance of the work from 1742–3; he then revised and published it in 1746. Again, the reason for writing: he was convinced that the Spirit of God was manifesting uncommon grace and favour. He was also confirmed in his belief that fanaticism had been the stumbling block of the revival, but with this added insight: excess was not only to be associated with the young and immature, but even more so with those who nurtured a 'false evangelical experience', those who put more value on bodily manifestations than on a changed heart. These were not those who relapsed to secular lifestyles, but, on the contrary, wanted to prolong the revival, celebrating and heeding 'impulses' and 'visions', regardless of their divisive consequences. These enthusiasts were so zealous that they would come under no one's authority of care and direction, and remained unsubmitted to the counsel of the Scriptures. With the issue clearly in focus, Edwards strikes at the heart: in a false conversion, one may have 'the corruption of nature only turned into a new channel instead of being mortified'. Great religious experiences, in and of themselves, are no sign or signal of true godliness. Conversion of heart is the only true distinguishing mark. For Edwards, the missing piece in those who are not subject to true grace is that of humility, 'one of the most essential things pertaining to Christianity' (I.295b). Elsewhere, he puts the issue pointedly: 'all gracious affections are broken-hearted affections' (I.302a).

In his preface, Edwards asks a simple question, one which he uses as a surgeon's scalpel to dissect revival phenomena: 'What is the nature of true religion, and wherein lie the distinguishing notes?' (I.235). Discernment of spirits continues to require his best efforts.

> In times of great revivals, as it is with the fruit-trees in the spring; there are multitudes of blossoms, which appear fair and beautiful, and there is a promising appearance of young fruit: but many of them are of short continuance; they soon fall off, and never come to maturity . . . In this world, [there never will] be an entire purity, either in particular saints, by a perfect mixture of corruption; or in the church of God, without any mixture of hypocrites with saints – or counterfeit religion and false appearances of grace with true religion and real holiness (I.235).

His purpose is not to repeat what he wrote in *The Distinguishing Marks of a Work of the Spirit of God*, but 'to show the nature and signs of the gracious operations of God's Spirit'. Edwards begins with an extended section, which, if updated, maps the laws of spiritual hydraulics. Increase the pressure in a person's life, and you discover what leaks out (I.237a). *Affection* is the term he chooses to describe the motivating, driving, inclining forces that are the source of our willing and acting. He maintains that the affections are the motivator in human life, 'the moving springs in all the affairs of life: take away all love and hatred, all hope and fear, all anger, zeal and affectionate desire, and the world would be, in a great measure, motionless and dead' (I.238a).

> True religion consists, in a great measure, in vigorous and lively actings of the inclination and will of the soul, or the fervent exercise of the heart. That religion which God requires, and will accept, does not consist in weak, dull, and lifeless wishes, raising us but a little above a state of indifference (I.237b).

In terms of our spiritual life, 'Doctrinal knowledge and speculation only, without affection, never is engaged in the business of religion' (I.238b). That, because 'the things of religion take hold of men's souls no further than they affect them' (I.238b). Several years earlier, in *Thoughts Concerning the Present Revival,* Edwards had written: 'An increase in speculative knowledge in divinity is not what is so much needed by our people as something else. Men may abound in this sort of light, and have no heat.' Rehearsing the unprecedented resources available by way of books, printed sermons and pamphlets, he then asks 'Was there ever an age, wherein there has been so little sense of the evil of sin, so little love to God, heavenly mindedness, and holiness of life, among the professors of the true religion? Our people do not so much need to have their heads stored, as to have their hearts touched' (I.391b). He uses the example of preaching . . . often there is no *e*ffect, because there is no *a*ffect.

> They [the hearers] remain as before, with no sensible alteration, either in heart or practice, because they are not affected with what they hear. I am bold to assert, that there was never any considerable change wrought in the mind or conversions of any person, by any thing of religious nature that ever he read, heard, or saw, who had not his affections moved (I.238b).

There follows a long contrast with the hard of heart, and the spiritually indifferent. But 'the Holy Scriptures everywhere place religion very much in the affections.' He draws out text after text on loving God with 'the whole heart'; on 'trembling with fear'; 'strengthening the heart, those that hope in the Lord'; of 'delight in the Lord'; of the call to 'rejoice, and be exceedingly glad'; on the broken heart, the contrite spirit.

He looks at David, 'a man after God's own . . . heart,' not brain.

The Apostle Paul, 'rejoicing with great joy', and the Lord Jesus . . . who again and again, 'was moved with compassion . . .'

Edwards concludes: 'These texts place religion very much in the affections. Those who maintain the contrary, must throw away what we have been wont to own for our Bible, and get some other rule to judge the nature of religion' (I.240a).

Edwards is absolutely convinced that Christian faith and experience cannot reside in intellectual understanding *alone*.[20]

[20] Iain Murray, *Op. cit.*, p.253.

> From a vigorous, affectionate, and fervent love to God, will necessarily arise other religious affections; hence will arise an intense hatred and a fear of sin; a dread of God's displeasure; gratitude to God for His goodness; complacence and joy in God when *He is graciously and sensibly present*[21]; grief when He is absent; and fervent zeal for divine glory (I.240a).

He uses the example of worship and praise: 'The duty of singing praises to God seems to be appointed wholly to excite and express religious affections' (I.242a).

Recalling the generating theme for these considerations, the nature of true religion, and its distinguishing notes, Edwards places at centre the following:

> That great work of God in conversion, which consists in delivering a person from the power of sin, and mortifying corruption, is expressed, once and again, by God's 'taking away the heart of stone, and giving a heart of flesh' (Ezekiel 11:19 and 36:26). Now, by a hard heart is plainly meant an unaffected heart, or a heart not easy to be moved with virtuous affections, like a stone, insensible, stupid, unmoved, and hard to be impressed. And what is a tender heart, but a heart which is easily impressed with what ought to affect it? (I.243a).

[21] Emphasis added.

Concluding this section that lays foundational bedrock, Edwards says,

> He who has no religious affection, is in a state of spiritual death, and is wholly destitute of the powerful, quickening, saving influences of the Spirit of God upon his heart . . . There must be light in the understanding, as well as an affected fervent heart; or where there is heat without light, there can be nothing divine or heavenly in that heart: so, on the other hand, where there is a kind of light without heat, a head stored with notions and speculations [but] with a cold and unaffected heart, there can be nothing divine in that light . . . If great things of religion are rightly understood, they will affect the heart (I.243b).

Edwards is still attempting to maintain a balanced position, facing the extremes of both detractors and zealous advocates: the following volleys are directed accordingly: 'They who condemn high affections in others, are certainly not likely to have high affections themselves' (I.244a) and,

> A man's having much affection, does not prove that he has any true religion; but if he has no affection, it proves that he has no true religion. The right way, is not to reject all affections, or to approve all; but to distinguish between them, approving some and rejecting others; separating between the wheat and the chaff, the gold and the dross, the precious and the vile (I.244a).

Building on his foundation, he moves on to give consideration to the bodily manifestations: 'True religion lies much in the emotions. There is great power in them and no reason exists why bodily sensations should not follow as a matter of course.'

> When the Spirit of power stirs our spiritual affections, such unutterable and glorious joys may be too great and mighty for weak dust and ashes, so as to be considerably overbearing it. The discoveries of God's glory, when given in a great degree, have a tendency, by affecting the mind, to overbear the body (I.246.b).

In '90s' terms, 'system overload', and in Vineyard-ese, 'Up comes the floor'.

'The Scriptures often make use of bodily effects to express the strength of holy and spiritual affections; such as trembling, groaning, being sick, crying out, panting and fainting.' (I.247a; Psalm 119:120; Ezra 9:4; Isaiah 66:2, 5; Habakkuk 3:16; Romans 8:26; Psalm 84:2). These manifestations, the 'affective excitements', are from the influence of the 'inward experience or sensible perceiving of the immediate power and operation of the Spirit of God' (I.248a). Describing the manifest presence of the Lord, Edwards says, 'It is God's manner, in the great works of His power, and mercy, to make His hand visible, and His power conspicuous.' He cites the exodus from Egypt, redemption under Gideon, David's conquest of Goliath, and the ministry of the early Church.

> And so it was with most of the conversions of particular persons recorded in the history of the New Testament: they were not affected in that silent, secret, gradual, and insensible manner, which is now insisted on; but with those manifest evidences of a supernatural power, wonderfully and suddenly causing a great change, which in these days are looked upon as certain signs of delusion and enthusiasm (I.248b).

Edwards never tires of reflecting on the *experience* of God's grace; the following is powerful enticement to spend some quiet time alone, meditating on the Scriptures:

> Holy affections are not heat without light; but evermore arise from some information of the understanding, some spiritual instruction that the mind receives, some light or actual knowledge. The child of God is graciously affected, because he sees and understands something more of divine things than he did before, more of God or Christ, and of the glorious things exhibited in the gospel. He has a clearer and better view than he had before, when he was not affected; either he receives some new understanding of divine things, or has his former knowledge renewed after the view was decayed (I.281b).

Implicit here is the critical issue of the source of inspiration, the 'roots', as we considered earlier. The experience of the manifest presence of God is always given, never produced.

> There is a great difference between these two things, lively imaginations arising from strong affections, and strong affections arising from lively imaginations. The former may be, and doubtless often is, in the case of truly gracious affections. The affections do not arise from the imagination, nor have any dependence upon it; but on the contrary, the imagination is only the accidental effect, or consequence of the affections . . . When the latter is the case . . . then is the affection, however elevated, worthless and vain (I.288b).

Self-generated religious experiences never produce fruit of any consequence. 'All gracious [true] affections arise from spiritual understanding . . . and spiritual discoveries are also transforming. They not only make an alteration of the present exercise, sensation, and frame of the soul; but such is their power and efficacy, that they alter its very nature' (I.302b). Edwards grounds this instruction on 2 Corinthians 3:18, where the Apostle declares, 'We all see as in a mirror the glory of the Lord, and we are being transformed into His likeness with ever increasing glory, through the power of the Lord who is the Spirit.'

This transformation in Christ leads to practical consequence. The end of the reviving work of God is 'Christian practice', and Edwards devotes the final three sections of his *Treatise on Religious Affections* to a delineation of the specifics called forth. The following can be considered as Edwards' conclusion:

Every tree is known by its own fruit.[22] Christ nowhere says, You shall know the tree by its leaves or flowers; or you shall know men by their talk, by their good story they tell of their experiences . . . or by many tears and affections . . . but by *their fruits.* Christ directs us to manifest our godliness to others. Godliness is as it were a light that shines in the soul: Christ directs that this light should not only shine within, but that it should shine out *before men,* that they may see it. But which way shall this be? It is by our good works. Christ does not say, that others hearing your good words, your good story, or your pathetical expressions; but *that others seeing your good works, may glorify your Heavenly Father* (I.321a).

A question that is frequently asked at the pastors' teaching time is, 'With all of the manifestations that have characterized the meetings at the Airport Vineyard, what assessment would Jonathan Edwards bring to bear?'

From his voluminous writings, I choose two final citations as my answer: both come from his *Thoughts on the Present Revival,* the most seasoned and comprehensive of all his writings on the Awakening. The first quote is Edwards' reply to an accusation brought against preachers who have 'made much of outcries, faintings, and other bodily effects; speaking of them as tokens of the presence of God, and arguments of the success of preaching; and

[22] Edwards cites Luke 6:44.

seeming to rejoice in it, yea, even blessing God for it when they see these effects.'

Edwards says:

> I have learned the meaning of (the manifestations) the same way that persons learn the meaning of language, by use and experience. I confess that when I see a great crying out in a congregation, in the manner that I have seen it, when those things are held forth to them which are worthy of their being greatly affected by them, *I rejoice in it*, . . . because I have found from time to time a much greater and more excellent effect.
>
> To rejoice that the work of God is carried on calmly, without much ado, is in effect to rejoice that it is carried on with less power, or that there is not so much of the influence of God's Spirit. For though the degree of the influence of the Spirit of God on particular persons, is by no means to be judged of by the degree of external appearances, because of the different constitutions, tempers and circumstances of men; yet, if there be a very powerful influence of the Spirit of God on a mixed multitude, it will cause some way or other a great visible commotion (I.394b).

The second citation comes from the first section of his *Thoughts on Revival*. Edwards begins his treatise by stating: 'They have greatly erred in the way they have gone about to try this work, whether it be a work of the Spirit of God or no, in judging . . . *the means and methods that have been used* . . .' He again states that it is not means, but the end that is of consequence:

> We are to observe the *effect* wrought; and if, upon examination of that, it be found to be agreeable to the word of God, we are bound to rest in it as God's work; and we shall be rebuked for our arrogance if we refuse [to acknowledge it as such] until God shall explain to us how He has brought this effect to pass, or why He has made use of such and such means in doing it . . . It appears to me that the great God has . . . poured contempt on all that human strength, wisdom, prudence and sufficiency which men have been wont to trust and glory in . . . so that the Lord alone shall be exalted (I.366ab).

CHAPTER FIVE

AN EMBARRASSMENT OF RICHES

Testimonies of Personal and Corporate Transformation

The Kingdom of Heaven is like this. A merchant looking out for fine pearls found one of very special value; so he went and sold everything he had and bought it.
(Matthew 13:45-46)

The biblical foundation for the experience of the manifest presence of God has been considered, and the theological reflections of Jonathan Edwards have brought critical insights to bear on the dynamics of renewal and revival. The title of this chapter arises from the thick file of written testimonies that nearly a hundred people submitted. I am deeply grateful to all those who have shared their stories; it has been a rich privilege to hear how the Spirit of God has met so many in so many beautiful ways.

Except for the brief biographical introductions, the following testimonies are first-person accounts, and have only been edited for syntactical purposes. The exception is the record of Sarah's experience; it was relayed to me by a family friend. All of the testimonies have been released for publication with permission.

It is now for the reader to 'test the spirits' in what is

reported in the following testimonies. Before proceeding, however, the great Baptist preacher, C.H. Spurgeon, offers counsel that may be of assistance.

> Observe how sovereign the operations of God are . . . He may in one district work a revival, and persons may be stricken down, and made to cry aloud, but in another place there may be crowds, and yet all may be still and quiet, as though no deep excitement existed at all . . . He *can* bless as He wills and He *will* bless as He wills. Let us not dictate to God. Many a blessing has been lost by Christians not believing it to be a blessing, because it did not come in the particular shape which they had conceived to be proper and right.[1]

Sarah Lilleman, *March 1994*

In October of 1991, 13-year-old Sarah caught what her parents thought was the flu. No sniffles and sneezes, however, could cause her eyesight, very poor from birth, to degenerate further; nor could the flu cause memory loss and cognitive dysfunction. Testing was done at Peel Memorial and Sick Children's Hospitals, Toronto, but no medical causes for her symptoms were found. As months passed, Sarah lost more and more muscle control, as well as cognitive ability. By October 1993, she was unable to walk, eat, swallow or see. In January 1994 she was transferred to Bloorview, a hospital for chronic care

[1] C.H. Spurgeon, *The Early Years, 1834–1859*, The Banner of Truth Trust, 1962, p.328.

patients, as she needed the aid of a mini-hoist to be put to bed.

On 27 February, 1994, Sarah's friend, Rachel Allalouf, came to the evening service at the Airport Vineyard. After Randy Clark's message, she received prayer, and while resting in the Lord, she had a vision of being at a table in heaven; her two grandfathers were there, as was Jesus. That vision 'faded' to one of the cross, where Jesus told Rachel to go to Bloorview Hospital the next day and pray for Sarah. Rachel reported that Jesus told her how to pray.

The next day, Rachel went to the hospital as instructed, along with her father, Simon. Sarah was in her special wheelchair – described as a 'stretcher on wheels'. She recognized the voices, but could not see or comprehend what was being said to her. Saliva was dribbling out of her mouth.

Rachel and Simon moved Sarah to a quiet place in the ward, where Rachel began praying the way Jesus had told her to. As she and her father interceded over the course of the next two and a half hours, Sarah began to cry, and then shake. Her sight began to come back, and her legs started to move. She slowly began to sit up on her own, and the previously uncontrollable drooling stopped. The joy of the Lord started to fill her, and Sarah was able to say, 'I'm getting stronger!'

Before coming to the hospital, Rachel was so convinced Jesus was going to heal Sarah, she had brought her friend a bag of dill pickle chips for her to eat. Over the next few days, Sarah began walking and eating on her own, even the chips! Her sight continued to improve.

Word of Sarah's recovery quickly went round the hospital. A few days later, a woman at the front desk came up to Simon and Rachel and said, 'The power of Jesus is real, isn't it?' She was a believer, and, as Simon reports it, 'was thrilled that the Lord had come and visited the hospital with His healing power.' She then asked them to pray for her alcoholic and unbelieving husband, which they did.

On 22 April, 1994, Sarah returned home from Bloorview – no one had any expectation that she would ever leave the chronic care hospital.

On Tuesday 26 April, Sarah was at the Airport meeting. Her friend Rachel was with her, and had received a further word from the Lord, that if Sarah would go to the front of the church and testify, He would heal her eyes. Sarah's mother noted how hard this was for Sarah, given her terrible fear of people – 'but she did it because she trusted God'.

One of the prayer team came forward, blessed Rachel, and then said to Sarah, 'Tonight you will have two healings from God – He will heal your eyes and He will heal your emotions.'

Sarah has since received further outpourings of the Holy Spirit such that she is able to pray in tongues. Her whole family has undergone radical change, is now closer than ever, and has a much closer walk with God. Simon's unbelieving wife came to the meetings at the Airport, and gave her life to the Lord early in May. Simon told an old friend of the Lord's work in Sarah's life, and he came to the meetings, and gave his heart to Jesus. Sarah's mother also brought a friend, and she too gave her life to the Lord.

Simon, a Messianic Jew, concludes his report: 'We just want to give all the praise and the glory to Jesus. We love Him with all our hearts and nothing, absolutely nothing is before Him. He is the Alpha and the Omega. Praise Yeshua!'

Ron Allen, *5 March 1994*

Ron is the founding pastor of the Fort Wayne Vineyard, and a Regional Overseer for the Association of Vineyard Churches. He has participated in over one hundred church plants, several of which have grown to membership of over a thousand. Before joining the Vineyard, he was the pastor of one of the largest Quaker churches in America. His wife Carolyn has given pastoral care to the churches they have served over the last twenty years. An accomplished musician, she moves prophetically as she ministers personally and corporately in the Church.

When I picked up the phone 3 February, John Arnott was on the other end. I could feel the intensity in his voice as he began relating to me what God was doing in their nightly meetings. His plea to 'come and check this out' was very appealing as he began to describe how the Holy Spirit was touching people. Randy Clark took the phone and began to describe how a four-day meeting had mushroomed into nightly meetings for three weeks, where hundreds were coming, and the Holy Spirit was falling in power on people, eliciting crying, laughing, shaking, falling down and jumping up.

My interest was stirred, and I bought a one-way plane ticket to Toronto.

As I was packing the Lord spoke to me and said, 'If you go to analyse, you'll end up criticizing, and I will lift my hand off of you. But if you go as a child to partake, I will pour out my anointing on you, again, and again, and again!' So I left my computer, took my Bible, and flew to Toronto that same day, Thursday, 3 February, 1994.

I arrived at the banquet hall where they were meeting, because they had outgrown their regular facilities, and I felt like I had walked into a bonfire. The worship was intimate, but very intense. Randy shared a short message and soon the laughing, crying and falling down was touching many.

I did the typical Vineyard pastor thing; I stood off to the side to observe what was going on. As Randy prayed his way through the crowd at the front, it was not long before he was standing in front of me. As he interceded for me, I felt this overwhelming sense of the peace and power of God come over me, and then it felt like someone turned out the lights. I don't know how long I was out, but I had this incredible sense of the immanent presence of the Holy Spirit resting on me. Throughout the evening, every time I would try to get up, someone would pray, 'Touch him again, Lord. More, Lord. More, Lord!' And out I would go again, each time resting deeply in the peace and presence of the Lord. I think it was around 3.00 a.m. when I finally managed to navigate my way out.

This went on for days. I felt and acted very intoxicated.

I couldn't talk, except in short cryptic phrases. I don't remember a whole lot, and I don't really want to believe the reports of how I acted! But as time passed I felt more and more cleansed and calm deep down on the inside. I felt the manifest presence of the Holy Spirit all the time, and continued to soak in a state of blissful abandonment.

I saw that this move of the Holy Spirit was not just a Vineyard thing. Many other denominations were represented in the evening meetings and the pastors' meetings. Evangelicals in particular were being powerfully encountered by the Holy Spirit. I witnessed people being healed of physical and emotional hurts, and I saw prodigals returning and recommitting their lives to the Lord. I saw pastors being refreshed and renewed.

Night after night the meetings grew. Soon there were protracted meetings in Hamilton, Cambridge, Stratford and Barrie. The same dynamic was being repeated in each place. Intimate worship, testimonies of God's touch upon people's lives, a message of grace, love and acceptance, an invitation to drink deeply of New Wine again and again; and then all the phenomena of people, young and old, being powerfully touched by God. A release of joy and celebration accompanied each ministry time which went on and on into the wee hours of the next morning.

Carolyn, my wife, joined me the last few days, and she soon was as drunk on the Holy Spirit as I was. When we returned to the office in Fort Wayne on Saturday afternoon, 12 February, one of the worship teams was in the auditorium practising. We stuck our heads in the door to say Hi, and the Holy Spirit hit the team; they were out on the floor, laughing and crying. We finally left so they could finish.

Sunday morning, 13 February, the Holy Spirit began to touch people immediately as we gathered for corporate worship. Soon everything we had seen in Toronto was happening in our fellowship. When it came time for the second service, we had to carry people from first service out into a side hall so we could begin again. But before we could open the service, the presence and peace of the Lord began to fall on the people as they came into the auditorium. We tried to follow a 'normal' pattern but before long we were praying for each other and God was graciously anointing all the people. Somewhere around 2.00 p.m. I announced an evening service which we normally don't have, and at 6.00 p.m. the building was packed. We worshipped, and then tried to share some of what we were experiencing; the Holy Spirit fell again, and we stacked up all the chairs to have room to minister as God continued to touch people till early the next morning.

We have been meeting nightly with about a third to half of the people joining us from other churches. About fifty pastors have been wonderfully touched by the Lord. This move has spread to nearby towns, and churches there have been taking nightly meetings. And so it goes on.

Some observations:

1 This move of God is bigger than the Vineyard. This is God's way of bringing His Church together to reach a city.

2 We get to keep all we give away.
3 If we come to observe we'll just have opinions, but if we come to participate, we'll receive a fresh anointing of the Holy Spirit and have Him to impart.
4 It seems that as long as leaders keep entering in, the people do too. People can ignore it or argue against it, but it doesn't seem to hinder what God is doing. We can't earn or demand it as a right, but we have to receive it as a gracious gift.
5 It takes humility to enter in and to continue to enter in. Those of us who have struggled with being controlling and bossy, have to bow down and come as children, laying aside all thoughts of prestige or position.
6 The worship, while intimate and intense, is punctuated by joy and delight. We've never really been a dancing church until now.
7 Unlike some models of ministry where the leader does it all up front, the ministry is being released to the Body. Even leaders are enjoying a kind of 'tag team' ability to hand off the leadership in the meetings without trying to hold on to control.
8 Evangelism is a steadily growing dynamic. People are witnessing boldly and enthusiastically about their relationship to Jesus Christ everywhere!
9 It's clear God is after a relationship, an intense love affair with His people. People don't watch TV or read the newspaper. They want to be with the Lord and each other.

10 Themes in the testimonies are the peace of God, the grace of God, the joy of the Lord, the healing touch of God, the Father-heart of God.

Our meetings are messy and a little scary, but then we've moved from the order of respectability to the order of anointing. This is not about a visitation, shortly to pass away, but rather that God is coming to His people to 'tabernacle' in them a deep, profound lasting way. God is coming *to* His people before He comes *for* His people.

More, Lord! More, Lord!

Carolyn's Testimony

As Ron left for Toronto to see what was happening up there, I remained in Fort Wayne wondering what this 'move of God' was all about. There were even moments I thought this might be just another conference or seminar and there might be some good information, but would God really be moving to make lasting changes in people's lives? This had been on my heart for a long time — 'Father, please come, live in Your people and change us. I'm tired of having more *goose bump experiences* that really don't change the way I am or live.'

Each time Ron called me from Canada, I felt an increase in the presence of the Lord just over the phone. Each time he had less to say; he would just cry and say, 'This is God.' By Sunday, the afternoon of the 6th, he could hardly speak at all. He was stuttering, with long pauses in between syllables. I was beginning to get concerned. This was not my articulate, verbose husband! Was this God or what?

As Ron was trying to talk to me the presence of the Lord was so strong he had to ask for help. He said, 'Randy (Clark) . . . H.h.e..e.l.l.l.p.p.p,' and then I heard a big thud. He had fallen to the floor, under the power of the Lord. I began to cry and shake on the open phone line; Randy talked to me for a bit, trying to explain what had been happening to Ron. I decided right then I was going to Canada the next morning and see for myself what was going on, and to partake of whatever the Lord had for me. I was hungry and thirsty for more of God. (I was also concerned that Ron had purchased a one-way ticket!)

I cancelled appointments, and left early Monday morning. On the way up all I could pray in my spirit was 'Whatever you want Lord . . . whatever you want.' I have to admit I was both scared and anxious. Would my husband ever be able to talk again? Had he flipped out, and gone over the edge? And if it was God, what would happen to *me*?

The Monday evening service was at the Cambridge Vineyard. When Ron walked in, I started down the aisle to greet him. He saw the pastor, Steve Stewart, first and went to greet him. They were both so drunk in the Holy Spirit that as they hugged they fell over in the aisle. I was awestruck.

We got Ron up and on a chair, and as worship began, he nudged me and pointed his finger in my face and said (as best he could) 'C..a..l..l 9 1 1.' There was a look of fear and distress on his face and it scared me. My first thought was he really had flipped out. As worship continued, Ron caught the eye of some others and said the same thing. It was so bizarre and so out of character we just laughed, mostly because we didn't know what else to do.

After a couple of days of Ron continuing to call for 911, someone finally put their hand on his head during a ministry time and said, 'It's OK, Ron. Jesus has heard your call for help (911) and He says it's going to be all right.' The peace of the Lord came over Ron then, and that was the last time he asked us to call 911.

Who can understand the ways of the Lord and our responses to Him? All along, way down deep in his spirit, Ron had just been crying out desperately for help. Jesus is the only One who can be that help, for all of us. We all desperately need Him touching us in our innermost being. I needed His touch and prayed once more, 'Whatever you want, Lord.' Seeing Ron receive as a child really helped release me to receive.

The Lord touched me so many ways in the last few weeks. I am continuing to be struck by the extremes of God's character and nature. I felt His power so strongly in my body one night, I became fearful that I was going to die; I have also felt an incredible presence of peace like never before. Even through all the manifestations of His presence and my body's response to them (i.e. shaking, shaking, and more shaking – one Baptist pastor observing me pray for people while I was trembling said, 'Isn't it great that the Vineyard lets the handicapped minister!'), this incredible peace is in the centre of my being. Could this be about learning of the abiding presence of the living Lord within His tabernacle – His people? The Lord is after an incredible love affair with us, and He wants everyone to be in on it.

Help us, Lord, to continue to respond to Your initiative, and to give away what You've given us so everyone will know of Your great love.

Postscript, 25 August, 1994

Seven months after our first visit to the meetings at the Airport Vineyard, God is still touching our lives in a powerful and overwhelming way. The 'entertainment' appeal has diminished somewhat as we're beginning to understand that the continued experience of God's manifest visitation is a call to abide in His presence more intimately and continuously, a more radical call to a devout and holy life, and an eager delight to share our faith with friend and stranger alike in a bold and spontaneous way. Last week we held tent meetings in the inner city. Not only did we see many healings, but over a hundred made first-time commitments to Jesus Christ. Fifty-five gang members gave up their caps and colours to follow Jesus Christ. More, Lord!

***Sarah,** 31 March, 1994*

For personal reasons, 'Sarah' has asked that her real name not be used.

I have been to over thirty Rodney Howard Browne meetings in an almost year-long pursuit of the Lord so as to restore the intimacy of relationship I once had with the Father. Meeting after meeting, I remained the only vertical one, so it seemed. If you start out feeling far away from God, you can imagine how it feels when it is practically proven time after time, month after month. Psalm 91:7 became my verse of the year. 'A thousand may fall at your side, ten thousand close at hand, but you it will not touch.'

Disappointed with the whole endeavour, I came up to Toronto only because of a strong sense of the Lord's leading. There, things turned. I want to thank the Airport Vineyard so very much for what they're allowing the Spirit to do there. It's very hard for me to receive, but the people there have been willing to spend the time and care I needed to begin to open up to the Holy Spirit again. They spent *hours* with me, and they wouldn't give up. They ministered so gently and compassionately that it began to feel safe again for me to receive. I haven't experienced love like this in many years.

The Lord came to me on the last night of my first stay, and overpowered me in such a way that I know His ability to give is greater than my unwitting ability to resist.

At first I just felt a good deal of energy flowing through me, and my body was involuntarily jerking now and then. It was extremely encouraging when Carol [Arnott] said she would stay with me while I was on the floor during the message. (If she hadn't said this, I'm sure I would have stopped what was happening and gotten up after a few minutes, just from self-consciousness.) Throughout the evening it seemed as if I could terminate what was happening, but at the same time it all seemed so unequivocally supernaturally empowered that I knew it was from the Lord. For that reason I dared not limit what God was choosing to do . . . at long last! Perhaps it required a setting safe enough to open up in and receive.

I don't remember too much of what Carol prayed, but I do recall that my body went into the most unusual motions in response to her prayers. Also, her words often elicited a deep response from my heart. After she prayed regarding birthing a prophetic mantle, my whole being seemed to go into labour – which proved exhausting. My head started to twist almost violently from side to side. While I worried this might throw my neck out, it actually loosened it up. (It tends to stiffen now and then from whiplash injuries.) As an expression of what I was sensing in my spirit, I remember motioning slowly with my hands in various ways I had never done before. Within seconds these motions became supernaturally empowered, *full speed ahead!* My hands and arms felt as if there was a power current running through them. Then there was the flailing, which I can't really describe except that my whole body seemed to be twisting on the floor, and someone later affectionately commented that I resembled the character 'Big Bird'. I remember thinking this seemed to be quite a workout for someone my age, and that perhaps this kind of anointing was supposed to be reserved for the 'under 30' crowd – but I was again glad finally to take what was given me!

At various times I did have to stop the intense bodily movements out of sheer exhaustion. Occasionally, the empowering just seemed to lift off momentarily, and I could rest. During these interludes I often sensed a sweet closeness of the Lord and/or the holiness of angels surrounding me. Actually the strongest sense of angels came when Carol prayed regarding worship and prophetic songs (the desire of my heart for years). At other times I would begin to weep at the manifest love of God, over the fact that He was not going to pass me by after all; that I was included in this renewal and restoration of His Church.

He showed me then that His blessing comes not by striving, but by grace on His part and trust and yieldedness on ours, in His time. During other 'rest periods' it was as if my whole being was caught up in worship, or crying out for more of Him (and less of me). But during the most intense physical manifestations, generally I was aware only of how strange the manifestation was, and how it seemed to follow from either Carol's prayers, the worship, or once or twice from something mentioned in the message (which I wasn't really listening to). Later, I rolled over and rested, feeling a bit like I'd just come out of general anaesthesia. With that, a feeling of spiritual 'sludge' inside me seemed to have been cleaned out in large part, and it was as if I could open up in a deeper way to the Lord. It was wonderful, and I'm so grateful, but want to go deeper still.

Later that night, something else very unusual occurred. A wave of extreme nausea came over me. At first I thought it might have to do with an inner ear disturbance from the violent head shaking, or perhaps dehydration. When several cups of water didn't help, my next fear was that it was demonic manifestation of some kind. Carol had prayed briefly concerning some deliverance, and I wondered if something had been stirred up. Because it had begun right after this encounter with the Spirit of God, while I was still on the floor, I felt it was spiritual in nature – I just wasn't sure which spirit was involved.

As I reflected on it, I remembered that the Lord had spoken to me only a few hours before the meeting, and had impressed upon me that there was something in my prolonged struggle to receive His blessing that was a bit like Jacob's struggle with the Angel of the Lord, and that when it came, I would be physically debilitated, not too unlike Jacob was. It also came to mind that Daniel was ill for several days after a supernatural encounter (Daniel 8:27). It seemed reasonable to me that if no man can see God and live, then something less than seeing Him fully could make us something less than dead, but none the less physically debilitated. While the nausea passed in a few hours, my arms were sore for two or three days from the shaking and flailing, but whenever I felt discomfort I just remembered why it was, and praised God!!

I was eager to see what difference there would be when I got back into real life. Our recent circumstances have been difficult and very discouraging, particularly with respect to the Messianic congregation which we moved to the — area to be a part of. But I now have an excitement about life with Jesus that I haven't experienced for several years. The Lord has taken me into a realm of grace that I've never before known: I'm actually just enjoying Jesus, and have the sense He's enjoying me. I'm not doing anything special at all for the

Kingdom, just loving Him and enjoying Him. Yet every day when I share with friends what God has done for me, and can do for them, the Holy Spirit comes; I feel His presence and others are touched simply out of the overflow of what He's done. And each day as I've prayed for people, they are touched in a way I haven't seen in many years. I prayed for a non-charismatic Lutheran neighbour earlier this week, and, without even telling her about the laughter in the Spirit, the instant I touched her belly and asked God to give her joy, she started laughing. It was wonderful to see the Lord give Himself to her! There's a new freedom and confidence in intercession, and during worship, words of praise and prophetic insight seem to well up and flow.

The Lord has also been doing a deep healing in my heart, relating all the way back to childhood. In all of this, He's been pouring His love and nourishment into me, and providing grace and understanding for forgiveness. I know there's no end to the healing/repentance/sanctification process, but I want so much for the garbage to be emptied so I can give myself fully to Him.

In summary, I feel that the Lord is restoring me to my first love with Him, only deeper because of all we've been through together. I'm so grateful for the role the Airport Vineyard has played in this, through their love and humility, by just allowing a place for the Spirit of God to move. I'm so grateful for the example of service and incessant giving to others. And I'm so very grateful for the Arnotts and the true pastors' hearts they've allowed Jesus to shape in them and those with whom they work.

I pray they'll be so richly rewarded they won't be able to stand it!

One last thing: I'm a Jewish believer and part of a Messianic Jewish congregation. The soonest I was able to schedule a trip to Toronto coincided precisely with Passover, which is the most significant celebration in our calendar. At first I hesitated to go and leave my family, but the Lord said that if I did, I'd know what deliverance from Egypt was really like. So I came and the Lord's word has proven true. How wonderful to go back home to celebrate the Resurrection refreshed in the Spirit, with a renewed understanding of His grace and an experience of true LIFE.

April 6 It's both easy and hard to write this expanded 'Part Two' thank you letter. It's easy because God has done so much that my heart overflows, yet hard because it's difficult to organize and condense so much overflow! In any event, this is a dilemma I'm content and happy to live with.

How can I thank God for finally setting me free to love and worship Him in a way I've ached to do for many years? For the grace just to enjoy Jesus (and even let Him enjoy me) for the first time in an 18-year-long relationship with Him? For the delight in watching others significantly touched merely by the overflow of my heart and life?

April 11 A few days have passed since the preceding page. To be honest, I've noticed that the 'high' has worn off. I don't know whether that's to be expected or not, and how much it might relate to our being in the process of extricating ourselves from an unhealthy congregational situation. Even so, there remains a deeper level of trust, peace and confidence in the Lord, and a greater sense of His leading and presence than before. I still wake up in the middle of the night feeling joyful, with a feeling of something like electrical energy all over me, and I lie there praising the Lord. I am a bit disappointed that the intensity has worn off, but pray that during this time He'll 'bring to completion' the things He said and did in Toronto.

In any case, I'm so glad they've decided to let the meetings go on and on . . . my limited experience shows me that getting filled once definitely isn't enough. We're able to return.

April 20–24 My husband and I are especially excited to be able to get filled up before our first overseas missions trip. (In May we're going to Moscow as part of an outreach aimed primarily at Russian Jews – who've been surprisingly extremely open to the Gospel.)

July 18 (Sarah returned to the Airport for a third visit.) The most far-reaching consequence of my recent week at the Vineyard was probably an expanded understanding of who God is, particularly the depth and breadth of His grace. With this has come a new, deeper sense of abiding in His rest and love. It was wonderful, and all I wanted to do was enjoy the Lord in all I did. I was at long last seeing that my rightstanding before the Lord began and ended with the completed work of Jesus Christ alone. Any of my attempted exploits for the Kingdom would never add to (or subtract from) this accomplished reality. They tried to teach me this in seminary; in fact, I think I managed an 'A' in the course, but never quite got the message.

When a much hoped and prayed for opportunity to participate in an evangelistic outreach to the Jews in Russia materialized shortly after my time at the Airport, I nearly declined to go. God could get the job done without me. Nonetheless, I eventually concluded that He was extending an invitation simply to follow Him into the harvest field. There was a strange new freedom in it all, leaving no room for even subtle self-promotion, as it was finally clear that works of service would not in themselves promote the worker. Just as strange was the realization that turning down the opportunity due to misunderstanding or fear would not condemn. The Lord had effected a major shift in my comprehension of His grace and calling on my life . . . and it was most liberating.

For nearly two decades I have laboured off and on in the field of Jewish evangelism, without much by way of tangible results. On this particular trip, however, our ministry team saw literally thousands of Jews (and as many non-Jews) coming to faith in Messiah! This kind of harvest was the fulfilment of a life dream, and is probably unprecedented in Jewish history. Time and again the Lord seemed to speak, lead, and open my eyes in the course of our ministry tour, just as He had been doing ever since Toronto.

In Russia, I touched a new joy that was even greater and deeper than the wondrous joys (including the holy laughter) that I had experienced at the Vineyard: that of entering into the joy of the Lord Himself at His own harvest. As I watched several thousand Jews turn to their Messiah, I was reminded of Jesus' desire to gather the children of Israel as a mother hen does her chicks. Two thousand years ago they were largely unwilling. This was a day, however, in which Jesus was visiting His people once more, and this time they were running eagerly to embrace Him. What overwhelming joy there is in the Lord's heart at the return of His people! And what matchless joy for us in entering into their homecoming as He shares His heart with His labourers! I have wondered whether this is what much of the present church renewal in North America will ultimately be about: the salvation of multitudes. If so, the best surely lies ahead!

As I reflect on my recent experiences, I observe the following changes in my life which I attribute directly to Toronto: the lifting of a depression that had lasted about two years; the substantial healing of a medical condition related to stress, oesophagal reflux, for which I was on strong medication; increased and sustained boldness and power in praying for others; more sensitivity to the Holy Spirit; freer worship; much diminished fear of others; and a renewed love relationship with the Lord. After years of feeling spiritually barren and shut away, the Lord has also recently opened doors regarding various ministry opportunities about which people at the Vineyard had prophesied as they prayed for me. But I have learned that any fruit borne from my time in Toronto persists only in the context of continuing to seek the Lord and abiding in Him on a daily basis. My experience is that there is a need for a *daily* infilling of the Spirit; a brief encounter does not cure or change all . . . but it's a marvellous jump start!

Happy Leman, *11 April, 1994*

Happy is the founding pastor of the Vineyard in Champaign, Illinois. He is the Regional Overseer for the Mid-West Region of the Association of Vineyard Churches. Before planting the work in Champaign, he was an insurance and estate planner, holding an M.B.A. from the University of Illinois.

On 18 March 1994, my wife Di and I felt that we were to go to Toronto so that we could experience firsthand the moving of the Holy Spirit. We had previously encountered Randy Clark in the fall of 1993 and were somewhat aware of what he was doing. At that time, we had believed that God was moving but we went to Toronto somewhat sceptical about the lasting impact of this outpouring.

The Holy Spirit did not allow our scepticism to last very long. Halfway into the first night, I was overcome by the power of the Spirit and found myself on the floor. After two hours of laughing, shaking, rolling and being unable to get up, I began to sense that the Lord was trying to get my attention. I realized that I had become very dry in my walk and that I was desperately in need of a refreshing. Throughout the weekend, Di and I were both touched many times.

We left Toronto convinced that God was indeed moving. It seemed the Holy Spirit was creating a new hunger for Jesus, a new desire for the Bible, a new boldness to share, an increased desire to pray, deeper repentance, and a host of other godly attributes. We were excited, as we believed that God had truly unleashed what we call an 'Acts 3:19 experience' – a time of refreshing.

While I was convinced that I had genuinely experienced God in Toronto, I had a nagging fear that I would be unable to bring this back to my church in Champaign. This fear was further increased by the testimonies that most of the other leaders who had been in Toronto were able to take it back in great measure and impact their churches. In fact, some of these men simply walked into their churches and people fell down.

As I walked into my church on Thursday, 24 March, no one fell, shook, laughed or cried. My tension rose slightly as I began to think that perhaps I didn't have anything to give away. These fears were quickly put to rest when we met with our staff Small Group that afternoon. We shared what had happened to us, and began to pray for the staff. For the next two and a half hours, the group was powerfully overcome by the Spirit. Some were on the floor laughing, crying, shaking, and experiencing other manifestations of the Holy Spirit. The next day, a young teenager walked into my office. I prayed for her briefly, and she fell under the power of the Spirit in the office hallway. Suddenly, it started breaking out among others in the office. I was now more encouraged.

On Saturday, 26 March, we had scheduled a healing seminar. We cancelled the programme and spent the entire four hours ministering to one another. I am now convinced we saw more of the works of Jesus by simply sharing and praying than we would have if we had taught the seminar. The next day, in our Sunday service, we saw a powerful outbreak of the Holy Spirit. Many people were touched with the same manifestations I had seen in Toronto. I realized God was indeed moving among us here at the Champaign Vineyard.

While most of the churches influenced by the Airport renewal have begun to hold protracted meetings immediately, we felt the Holy Spirit was instructing us differently. Our leading was to divide the pastoral staff into teams of two or three and send them into the Small Groups. In this way, we were able to minister to everyone in the group as well as answer questions. It seems that we've been able to overcome many of the fears that people had when they were simply watching on Sunday morning.

Our experience in the Small Groups has been eye-opening to say the least. For example, the first group was one that we knew would be hesitant about these supernatural events. In fact, several of the group's members said they didn't like what had happened in church and were not open to it in this particular meeting. The individual most opposed watched quietly for about two hours. Then, somewhat reluctantly, he agreed to allow someone to pray for him and soon found himself thrashing wildly on the floor for over an hour. At the close of the meeting (after midnight), he admitted that indeed God had impacted him in such a way that he would never forget it. In fact, it seemed that Jesus had immersed him in such love that all he could see or think about was Jesus.

This type of scenario has happened in Small Group after Small Group. In every meeting the Holy Spirit has displayed His mighty power. Our youth and children's Small Groups are included, for they are seeing the same things.

Now, just two weeks later, the Small Groups are supernaturally ministering to each other regularly without the pastors present. To us, this is a major breakthrough in that the people are being empowered by the Holy Spirit to release ministry as He gives it.

Postscript: 23 August, 1994

The easiest way to describe the last five months is by using the last verse of John's Gospel: 'There is much else that Jesus did. If it were all to be recorded in detail, the world could not hold the books that would be written.' We have seen lives ***radically*** changed – physical healings and restorations, and emotional and relational transformations. We have an awesome God!!!

Melanie Morgan-Dohner, *May 1994*

Melanie and her husband are associate pastors at the Hopkinsville Vineyard, and have served there as psychotherapists for the last two years. Melanie is mother to Monica – since kindergarten, Monica has had a recognized learning disability.

In late February, nine people from the Vineyard Christian Fellowship in Hopkinsville, Kentucky, came to the Toronto Airport Vineyard, to soak in what God was doing there. One of those people was Heather Harvey, 13-year-old daughter of Graham Harvey, our Senior Pastor.

Heather has struggled with dyslexia for her entire school career. From her early youth, she had problems processing what she heard, and understanding both spoken and written words. Reading has always been very difficult. She often felt 'left out' because of her inability to understand much of a conversation; she found it very hard to understand directions.

In Toronto, she asked for prayer for her learning disability. We had been there four nights, and had been getting ministry at every opportunity. Heather had many times, during and after prayer, shaken and jerked, and sometimes done dramatic dance-like movements. When she received the prayer for dyslexia, she fell to the floor, very still.

Later she told us that angels had done brain surgery. She heard God instructing them, and was told to be very still because 'this is very delicate surgery'. She also reported that one of the angels got so excited that she began playing with Heather's brain, and that God had to calm her down, saying, 'This is very serious, and not the time for play.' (She thought that was funny.) She felt herself on a cold operating table, and at the end, saw a picture of herself praying for other friends with dyslexia.

The night we arrived home from Toronto, Heather

excitedly headed straight to my daughter, Monica, who also is dyslexic, and prayed for her. Later Monica told me this story: 'The angels shaved my head, across the top of it, from ear to ear. Then they cut my head, pulled the front of it open, and took out my brain.' She drew a picture of how her brain had looked, with a concave, indented area. 'That is what the angels worked on, pulling that out to be curved, like the rest of my brain. Then they put it back in my head, and I could feel the tug of stitches, across the top of my head.'

Her reading tutor says, 'No question . . . the dyslexia is gone!' Monica still has to catch up on all the things that she's been unable to learn, but she says every day, 'I *understood* what was happening in school today!'

That's how it began. Heather, Monica and Monica's sister, Autumn Morgan-Dohner, began praying for anyone who had dyslexia. Heather and Autumn both have been able to watch the angels' movements during what they all refer to as 'brain surgery'. The adults have stood by, and watched, but stayed out of their way!

Heather Harvey, *13 years old*

Heather reports that she can understand school much better. She says that she can now memorize things, and recall them. While it used to take her a long time to comprehend word problems, now they, and directions, are understandable.

Her mother, Mary Harvey, says that reading seems much easier for Heather; she is not making 'dyslexic-type' mistakes now, such as reversing letters, and missing the first sound of words. She saw an immediate difference in Heather's typing skills, as the dyslexic 'reversals' of letters caused many mistakes, and used to slow her down so much. Her speed and accuracy has picked up quickly. Most of all, her mother sees that an excitement about learning is replacing the fear from confusion; Heather is also developing the joy of reading.

Monica Morgan-Dohner, *11 years old*

Monica's school grades have immediately improved. Her reading tutor reports that, like Heather, she has much to learn in order to catch up to grade level, but now she has the ability to do so. She sounds out words beginning with the first letter, when previously she would sound out the middle or ending letters (seeing those as the first letters). Monica had been very concerned about going to Middle School next year, fearful of not being able to keep up; that fear is subsiding as she continues to be amazed at her ability to focus, listen to detail, and understand things going on around her.

At home, we now see her reading voluntarily, carrying books around, and bringing a book for a long ride in the car. None of this ever happened before her healing. She is interested in joining in on the Sunday School work that involves reading and writing, and previously she would have never even looked at it. We delight in the new possibilities ahead for Monica.

Sammy Collins, *12 years old*

Sammy did not see or hear anything during the prayer.

Autumn, however, saw angels working in his brain, and saw them take a piece from one side of his brain and move it to the other side. He has had much difficulty reading and learning, and says that before he would not read in front of anybody, but now he does. His teachers say his reading is really improved. He does not see words backwards any more!

Tina English, *13 years old*

A peer of Heather's, Tina had also struggled all through school. While Heather, Autumn and Monica prayed for her, she saw angels doing something to her brain that seemed like 'they were kind of fiddling around with it'. She had a headache of short duration following the prayer.

She found school to be considerably easier afterwards, and her grades improved significantly. She passed her grade level, and plans to spend part of the summer working on learning words that she couldn't learn before. She reports that before her healing, she could not concentrate long, and had problems of not being able to remember or understand things she had read. Now, her reading is easier, faster, and she retains what she's read.

Cindy English, *adult*

Tina's mother, Cindy, also wanted healing. When Heather, Monica and Autumn prayed for her, she cried and felt sad. The deep pain from her school days was called up, having been called 'dumb' at home and at school, and never being able to keep up in class, or even comprehending the depth of what she was missing. She remembered being made to stand in the hall outside the classroom, as punishment for not having understood something; she was completely confused as to what had happened.

Her impression after the prayer was that God needed to do a lot of inner emotional healing before touching the dyslexia, and that she would need to get prayer some other time for the learning disability. Some time later, however, she found herself really interested in a book she had wanted to read, and even read parts of it out loud to her husband. They both realized what an unusual thing that was. They began to suspect that 'something had happened.' Cindy used to have difficulty with recall, reading only four or five pages before having to go back and read them again. She has been reading up to eighty pages a night now, and retaining the information. With her comprehension problem, she had previously concluded that reading was a waste of time for her. She is now excitedly talking about her discoveries in books.

Given that she suffered longer than the children, she rejoices all the louder for her healing!

We have seen over and over that the Lord really honours and blesses us when we go in search of what He's doing. If there is any other information we could provide, please call us. We have LOTS of stories to tell about what God is doing.[2]

[2] Melanie Morgan-Dohner, P.O. Box 754, 1015 Skyline Drive, Hopkinsville, Kentucky, 42240; ph. 502–885–7414.

***Belma Vardy**, 20 July 1994*

Belma is an accomplished dancer, teacher and choreographer, and travels throughout Canada, the U.S., and Europe, conducting dance and worship workshops and seminars for churches of many denominations. She has taken part in worship conferences such as America Arise, Canada Arise, Ministering Arts Conference, and the International Dance Conference in France. She has produced a worship tape titled 'Songs for a Celebration of Dance'.

On Sunday afternoon, 23 January, I accompanied a friend to the Airport Vineyard. The purpose of the trip was to drop off a letter, and when we arrived, an unexpected sight greeted us. The church service was definitely over, but there were some people rolling all over the floor, laughing hysterically, I sat down at the back of the church and watched, keeping my distance.

I thought, 'This can't be for real; these people are just looking for attention.' When I saw the pastor's wife, Carol Arnott, on the floor laughing, I was shocked and appalled at her behaviour. I thought it was so undignified. I was full of criticism and mistrust. I thought, 'I'm so glad I don't attend this weird church.' It is an understatement to say that what I had witnessed did not fit my Christian Reformed Church grid!

I was standing right near the door ready to leave when someone came and asked me if I had been prayed for. I said that I hadn't, and found myself thinking, 'One thing I can always use is prayer. If this is You, God, I'll receive whatever You have for me. If there is anything here that is not of You, then, God, don't let it come on me.' The next thing I knew there were about ten people surrounding me. As they started to pray for me, I felt a heat penetrate through my face. I felt as if the Lord's face was right against mine, and it seemed as though His love began to fill me.

The prayer time was such a good experience that I decided to go back and attend one of the services to see what the special meetings were all about. I am, by nature, an analytical person, and don't accept anything readily without checking it out first. During the months that followed, I went, on average, three times a week to observe the goings on, fascinated by it all but not totally convinced that it was God. I myself did not experience any of the outward manifestations I was witnessing, but I did notice some changes in my attitudes, and the ways in which I relate to the people in my life. I found myself forgiving with greater freedom, and, at the same time, became much more aware of things for which I needed to repent. This most often happened in my private quiet time when alone with the Lord; this too had changed, as I have developed a greater hunger and thirst to know God in a more intimate way. As these things were taking place, I started to believe that what I was witnessing at the Airport was indeed a move of God, and I became more open and receptive to all that was going on.

I shared with a friend what was happening at the Vineyard, and talked about some of the deep changes that had taken place in my heart. On 22 March she accepted an invitation to go with me to the meeting, but before we arrived, she asked if any of the manifestations would happen to her. I assured her that she was safe. 'Nothing will happen to you; I've been going for weeks, and nothing has happened to me by way of the manifestations.'

As usual, the worship that night was wonderful. Pastor John gave the announcements, and I noticed that a friend on my left was making strange noises and slight jerking movements. It looked like he was trying to hold back laughter. I had never seen him act like this before; he seemed embarrassed about what was happening to him. I pointed him out to my girlfriend. He surprised us both by bursting into hysterics. We didn't understand what was happening. All of a sudden it was as if the heavens opened up and a bucket of laughter was dumped on the two of us as well. We burst into uncontrollable laughter. It overwhelmed us and we just howled with laughter. No matter how we tried, we couldn't stop – it was totally out of our control. My girlfriend fell over sideways, and I fell on her with my head on her hip, so unladylike. We unsuccessfully tried to sit up and regain our composure, but as soon as we sat up, we fell over. When I tried to pull myself up on to the chair seat, I ended up on the floor between two rows of seats. My girlfriend was lying across the seats and crawling along them like a worm, laughing hysterically and trying to get away from me. It seemed that every time we touched each other, it set us off again in uncontrollable hysterical laughter until we were snorting and laughing so loudly we were disturbing the meeting. To us it seemed there was a wall of silence around us; we could see someone speaking, but we couldn't hear him. It was as if we were at our very own little party.

At the end of the evening we literally crawled out on our hands and knees. We were not at all embarrassed, and didn't care what we looked or sounded like. In fact, everyone seemed to think it was quite normal for us to leave this way! I have always been very prim and proper, so this was totally out of character for me.

The next morning, I woke up feeling so full of the presence of God. I felt refreshed and rejuvenated, and had a deeper love for my heavenly Father. That evening my friend and I decided to go back – this time we wore ski pants!

Before the meeting, I had said to the Lord, 'Whatever it takes to change me and make me more like You, I am open. I'm Yours.' Pastor John called me up to testify as to what God had been doing in me the night before. It was totally unexpected, and I found myself unable to speak. I opened my mouth but no words came out. This continued for about five minutes, and set the laughter off again. The ministry team prayed for me, and I fell to the floor without even being touched.

As I lay on the floor that night at the Airport Vineyard, I felt a beautiful presence come all over me. I lay there for three hours, something which I had never done before – at least not in church! As I lay there, I felt my physical body unable to get up, and as I 'rested', I had what I best describe as an 'out of body' experience.

I saw myself walking in a lush green pasture, hand in

hand with Jesus. We came to a river and He told me that this was the 'River of Life which flowed from the Throne of God' (Revelation 22:1). The first part of the river was very shallow, about a foot deep. As we walked further into the river, I noticed the water flowing *through* my leg, not around it. As we continued to walk I felt a refreshing feeling flow through my body from my toes up to my head.

After the three hours I struggled up and had to be driven home. That night I was woken up at 2 a.m. Immediately upon opening my eyes I was wide awake. I heard a voice say, 'Look at your leg.' [Since July 1988, I have had a growth on my leg. It started out with what seemed like a rash, but by March 1994 it covered an area of approximately four inches in length and two inches in width, raised to about 1/16 of an inch, and was extremely irritating, itchy and painful. I had been to the doctor many times over the six years, and was told that it was a skin condition which I would have for life. The doctor essentially said that there was nothing they could do for me.]

I knew immediately to look at the leg where the growth was. It was TOTALLY GONE! I gasped and started touching the spot, rubbing it, totally in awe. It was so smooth – it looked like new skin. I thought I was dreaming – 'Where did it go? Lord, what happened?' On awaking that morning, I had the proof that it was not a dream, and marvelled at the healing. I found it very hard to digest – that God would love me so much as to heal me.

That night I had a dream. The dream re-lived all that I had experienced the previous night, lying on the Airport's carpet. I was again walking in heaven, hand in hand with the Lord. We came to the river and He said, 'This is the River of Life. In it there is healing. As we were walking through it you were healed. My child, I love you; receive my love.' At that moment I woke up crying.

Some time later, I made an appointment with my doctor to have my leg examined. He checked where the growth had been; the nurse looked, and then checked my chart; I had indeed been in many times before, and repeatedly had a medicated cream prescribed. Both the doctor and the nurse marvelled, and said that I was very lucky, that skin conditions like I had do not usually go away. They asked what had happened, and I shared my experience with them, and told them that I was certain that God had healed me. The nurse said, 'I believe you, Belma; I feel a real stirring inside as if something really exciting is about to happen. It's almost like the medical and spiritual are coming together as one!'

I left the doctor's office thanking the Lord for His presence with me, and for the opportunity to give testimony to the doctor and nurse. I give the Lord Jesus Christ all the glory for His grace and mercy poured out on me!

There are many other wonderful stories of what God has done in my life this year since the renewal has begun. I still attend an average of two meetings a week. I have dropped all expectations of what may or may not happen, and allow myself to be drawn into the presence of Jesus. I have not had any further physical manifestations, but they themselves are not as significant as the Sovereign working of God's Spirit in my heart – especially a deep repentance – with loads of grace; I *know* that God meets me where I'm at.

I have a new love for the Lord, much deeper than ever before, and with it, a desire and thirst to draw close to Him, a hunger to get to know Him. I want to lose sight of self and totally surrender myself to Him, and get to know His will for my life. All I want is His Substance, His Presence, His Strength, His Agenda and His Purpose for my life. I have found that I have a deeper trust in Him, and a much deeper understanding of how much He loves me. I have a new passion to read His Word, and as a bride in love with her bridegroom, so I have felt myself falling in love with Jesus all over again.

The laughter has hit me four times in my home. As I surrender and submit to Him, and allow Him to mould me, He fills my empty heart over and over again and covers me with His power and His glory. It is there in my time alone with Him that He refreshes and energizes me, and puts life back into me once again. One morning, the Lord impressed upon me the *truth* of Ecclesiastes 3:14: 'I know that whatever God does lasts forever; there is no adding to it, no taking away. And He has done it all in such a way that everyone must feel awe in His presence.'

Terry Bone, *5 August 1994*

Terry is thirty-seven years old, married with three children, and has been in full-time ministry for eight years; for the last two he has served a church in Grimsby with an average Sunday morning attendance of about 125. He grew up in a home with only nominal church affiliation, and became a Christian in his teenage years at a Brethren Bible camp. He attended a 'Jesus People' group, married a Spirit-filled Lutheran minister's daughter, and has served the Pentecostal church.[3]

In January 1994, our church was experiencing some of the typical 'transition' difficulties in ministry. This process began to bring some of my own long-standing personal issues to the surface of my life, and I didn't particularly like what I saw.

In February, I received two separate long-distance phone calls from friends who had heard about what was happening at the Toronto Airport Vineyard. Both indicated that they felt God had directed them to call me and that I should check out what was happening. My response at the time was 'That's good for them, but the Lord knows where I am and if He wants to bring revival to Grimsby, Ontario, I'm here waiting.' I thought I was being spiritual by not running after someone else's blessing.

By March, I recognized that my ministry effectiveness had shrunk to the level of maintenance based upon human effort alone. Although still conducting regular intercessory prayer meetings, there was a definite 'power shortage' in my life.

I confess that even though I am Pentecostal, over the

[3] Terry Bone, Lakemount Worship Centre, 54 North Service Rd. Grimsby, Ontario, ph. 905–945–8888.

years I had developed an aversion to overt manifestations of the Spirit because I have seen so much that did not seem real. On two occasions I had been 'pushed' down by someone a bit too eager to see me 'slain in the Spirit'. In contrast, services I led were marked by order and punctuality. My business background in computer systems analysis seems to have determined an analytical approach to every area of my life, including the 'things of the Spirit'!

In March, my denomination executives called a special prayer meeting for pastors. During this time, while praying with my eyes closed, the Lord showed me a picture of my soul, after which I saw a large hand come down and remove something marked FEAR. At that moment, I perceived that the Lord was removing from me the fear of that which is phoney, and the fear of loss of control – which, for me, go hand in hand. A few seconds later, I fell backwards on to the floor where I stayed for over half an hour weeping, while the Spirit of God did some inner healing. I wasn't very orderly that day.

Several weeks later, I went to the Wednesday pastors' meeting at the Airport Vineyard. I joined local pastors in the café adjoining the sanctuary, and after brief introductions, two Baptist pastors, a United Church minister, a Bible College teacher and a couple of Vineyard leaders (none of whom I had met before) gathered around my chair and began to pray quietly. Immediately, one prayed with an insight which I believe was given directly by the Spirit. Another broke bonds of unbelief and another prophesied about my life and church. The presence of the Spirit was so heavy upon me that I finally fell off the chair on to the floor. These determined men were persistent; one prayed 'More fire, Lord,' and my body tensed as I felt a strange sensation throughout. It seemed that God was doing something to me so deep within that I could not comprehend.

I was not 'out of control'. I did not fear any of this and had the feeling that I could stop this experience at any time – but I didn't dare try.

That same night I returned to my home church to lead a planning meeting for our church picnic. I didn't preach, I didn't pray, I didn't include any music or worship. We simply discussed such mundane matters as who cooks the food and who cleans up. When I tried to close the meeting with a simple prayer, the Holy Spirit said clearly to me 'There's work to do.' I related these words to the twelve people at this meeting and we all just waited silently in prayer. Within a few minutes, powerful physical manifestations began, and by the time we finished an hour and a half later, some had fallen to the floor, one was dancing with joy, one quiet and reserved lady began to laugh, and others wept with the release of the Spirit from deep within. We left amazed and blessed.

Over the next three weeks, I kept returning to the Airport Vineyard to 'continue to soak' as they like to say. Back at our home church, each service brought new delights and surprises. The day before our services on Sunday, 5 June the Spirit clearly spoke to my heart saying 'I want to bring fire'.

'OK Lord,' I responded, 'I'll try to get ready.' First I scrapped my planned message (that never comes easy), and then I quickly did a computer Bible search on the word 'fire'.

That night at home my wife expressed some reservations about some of the recent manifestations, especially to do with falling and laughing.

The next morning I preached the 'fire' sermon, and the ministry time following was marked by one lady collapsing upon another in outbursts of laughter. Then, at the end of the evening service 'all heaven broke loose' upon us. I made a simple call to the front for anyone who would like prayer. About forty people came forward. I stood back playing my guitar while I watched bodies drop. My previously cautious wife was gripped with profuse laughter from the Spirit, went down on the floor and couldn't get up for two hours. The assistant pastor's wife began to quiver and moan and fell to the floor beside my wife. For the next two hours, when one would moan, the other would laugh! Later on my twelve-year-old son came forward and said 'I think kids can receive too, Dad'. As soon as he raised his hands, he began to sob, fell to the floor, and soon after began to laugh louder and longer than ever in his life. After thirty minutes, he began to flow with Spirit-given language for the first time! This was followed by my ten-year-old daughter falling to the floor and remaining there, hands extended upward, praising God.

During the course of the evening, my wife was given a picture by the Lord of our sanctuary as an operating room for the Spirit, with those praying over others resembling nursing attendants.

Over the next two weeks, we made room for this kind of ministry two nights per week. I was present at every meeting and was amazed to see people, whom I know well, acting out of character, yet seemingly receiving exactly what God had in mind for them. These experiences have begun to produce real fruit. One Sunday morning I asked for testimonies in our service. One man, who had just had his first 'carpet experience' at the Airport Vineyard, stood and confessed how the Lord had removed resentment from his heart toward his pastor (that would be me – standing beside him with the microphone), and toward other family members. Many testify about personal renewal, renewed passion for the Lord and improved personal relationships. Several have spoken of increased faith and it is evidenced by their willingness to pray for others and serve in church ministries.

Over the months, we have witnessed many unusual responses to the power of the Spirit – BUT – when the manifestation referred to as the 'Lion's roar' began to occur at the Vineyard, I decided that this move of the Spirit had finally begun to slip off the rails and was in danger of becoming weird. I felt that I had reached my limit. For a brief period, I began to back off my habit of 'seeking and soaking' (calling out to God personally for more power and attending services where His power was manifestly present). As a result, *it was ME who began to slip off the rails.*

Upon my return to the pastors' meetings at the

Airport, I joined the group in the café *in order to pray for others* but once again these Spirit-led men converged upon me. Earlier that day I had remarked how I didn't feel the need for some of the overt manifestations and never expected them to happen to me. But now, as they quietly prayed for me, the Lord began to reveal an area of my life that was still ruled by 'self'. This was followed by an unexpected 'roar' of faith welling up within me. It increased until I had to give vocal expression. When I did, I sensed that Jesus, *the Lion of Judah*, was within me, literally chasing out the power of sin and declaring His righteous anger at the remaining captivity of my soul. This was followed by prophetic utterance and a shaking of the right side of my body which lasted for nearly an hour.

The result of this experience? I mark an increase of faith and a boldness to speak prophetically, and an increased anointing upon my ministry as I pray for people – the Holy Spirit comes in power as never before.

It has amazed me how unknowable are the ways of God. Why would I need to experience these strange but wonderful manifestations in order to see my ministry increased and the Spirit released? I still have a teaching ministry, *but it now often focuses upon explaining what God is doing rather than teaching what we hope He will do.* Our God seems bigger and our problems seem smaller. God is giving each of us what we need, even when we don't know what that is!

We are training persons to minister effectively during ministry times and are planning some more special meetings. What else can I say?

'COME, HOLY SPIRIT!'

***Alan Wiseman**, 8 August 1994*

Over the last three months my spiritual life has heated up dramatically. I have tried to keep a written record of what God has been doing in my life, but it has been really hard to keep up. He seems to be speaking to me, acting through me, and moving in the lives of those around me at an unprecedented speed. I praise God for what He has been doing, and pray that His power to change me into Christ's likeness will continue and even increase, so that Jesus will be glorified in me more and more every day until I see His face.

I am the son of missionary parents, and was born in South Africa. I am a classically trained musician and have worked for over ten years as a music director in two Baptist churches and a Presbyterian church. My education includes a degree in music, and one in theology from Ontario Theological Seminary. For many years I have admired, from a distance, what God has been doing in the Vineyard Churches, but I have never been drawn to join them or even associate with them. I was waiting for something different.

When I was a teenager, a missionary woman in South Africa prayed for me and I was filled by the Holy Spirit and received the gift of tongues. Because my family and church were very hostile towards what they perceived to be the divisive gifts of the Spirit, I kept this blessing to myself. I have always worked and worshipped in conservative evangelical churches which do not operate in the more supernatural gifts of the Spirit, and so I generally tried to keep secret the dreams, visions and prophetic words that I was receiving. I have even experienced the laughing of the Spirit we now see at the Vineyard, but it was years earlier, and I was all alone at the time.

For years I have prayed for renewal within the conservative environment to which I have been called, but I always had this dilemma: I wanted a charismatic church where I would be free to express all the gifts I felt God had given me, but I also wanted an intellectual and aesthetically sophisticated environment. I guess I wanted a *charismatic high church*. It seemed to me that the charismatic churches I knew of were led by people without a great deal of education, who worshipped with music that was simplistic and aesthetically unpleasing. I chose to stay where I was and to continue to pray that God would renew the traditional churches with the same power that was evident in the Vineyard, and so allow us to discover a form of the charismatic renewal which would be more viable for the culturally sophisticated (forgive me for the dreadful superiority).

On 31 March 1994 I went to the Airport. I had heard from friends that God was moving there in power and that there were many manifestations of His presence. When we arrived, we met some mutual friends and, like good Baptists, sat with them near the back. What I witnessed at the meeting bombarded my senses. I heard people laughing, I saw people shaking, and I felt quite confused. About an hour into the meeting, I left for a while and went down the street to a coffee shop. I was so overloaded with what I was witnessing that I wanted some time to think with just normal people around me. A short time later I came back to the meeting: we stayed until they began to pray for people, and then we left. Both my wife and I felt quite sure what we had witnessed was the power of God, but I was sure that it was being mismanaged. I felt that everything was entirely too casual and unorganized, and I really did not like the music.

Once I had been convinced that what I was seeing at the Vineyard was from God, it was a humbling step for me to say, 'Lord, I believe this is You. I want more of You, and if I must shake in order to receive, then I will shake. Please bless me.' Praise God, I have received from Him what I desired, and praise Him even more that I have been humbled to receive this from the Vineyard to the accompaniment of bizarre behaviour.

Over the next few months, I used any excuse I could find to go back. I have received prayer from the Airport ministry teams many times and have been greatly blessed by it. The Spirit's power has been dramatically – sometimes violently – manifested in my body through shaking, laughing, crying and roaring like a lion! I do not really like to think of any of these experiences as being the consequence of receiving something brand new. Yes, new things have happened to me since I went, but this is because I received *more* of what I already had. I received a flood of the Spirit's power into my life – my poor body has had a hard time containing it all – I have had sore muscles for weeks! I perceive the activity of God in this renewal rather more like an intensification and increase of His work in my life up to this point. When I was prayed for at the Vineyard, the work of God in my life speeded up at an incredible rate. I had been growing in the gift of prophecy before I went, but afterwards the gift has become much more powerful. There are now physical manifestations that accompany the original gifting, stirred up to such an extent that the power is so strong, my limbs shake with it! I am thankful not so much for the new manifestations, as for the new power.

For some people the manifestations might be something highly desirable. This has not been the case for me. The manifestations have been very awkward and humbling. In the conservative circles in which I move, it is very troublesome to have dramatic manifestations accompanying your ministry! For example, shortly after I was prayed for, I sat at my computer typing the church bulletin, and in the course of copying the order of service, I typed the words, 'Come, Holy Spirit'. I was immediately thrown into a fit of shaking, and bounced around on my wheeled office chair! These sorts of manifestations are often intrusive! I have had to learn to laugh and thank God for them.

Over the course of these last few months, I have discerned a mysterious sense of logic and meaning in the shaking movements. When I am under the Spirit's power and start to shake, I find that my body is highly responsive to the Spirit's desires and actions. The shaking seems to be the Spirit's power, but *how* I shake seems to represent what He is doing. If the Spirit desires to fill someone, my arms fly in circular motions; if He desires to break bonds, my arms start chopping. There is an extensive repertoire of kinetic language that seems to symbolize the Spirit's desires and actions. I am humbled and amazed at the ways of God.

Each experience of the presence of the Holy Spirit's power has been very rich with meaning for my life; however, it would take far too long to relate them all. I would rather talk about the changes in my heart and the new understanding I have of God's activity in His Church. I had, over the course of the last two years, been learning about Christ's strength in me. He had given me the courage to do things for Him that I had formerly been too weak to accomplish. That strength has been greatly increased, and God has prophetically manifested it in me by making me roar like a lion. As I was prayed for and began to roar the first time, I felt an incredible rush of lion-like strength which was a very pleasurable feeling. I seemed to be feeling the invincibility of Christ. This sense of Christ's strength was also combined with a sense of His anger at his foes, and a knowledge of their imminent demise.

This new power I have experienced as a flow of God's love into my life seems almost electrical. It quickens my love for God, and my love for others. It intensifies my desire to minister, and my satisfaction in doing so. It empowers my spiritual gifts, stirring them up and fanning them into flame. I guess I could call this added power 'a new anointing' by the Spirit. This is something that we all desperately need. We may not all need to shake, but we all need His love and power.

I have already said that I feel I have received an increase in the power of my spiritual gifts, and an increase of Christ's strength in me; let me also tell of the most precious gift that I have yet received.

I have, since I was young, led a fairly disciplined spiritual life. I struggled hard to love Christ more than anything else and to put Him first. But I also struggled with very powerful desires to sin. He has granted me a fair amount of victory, but it has always been a struggle. When this work began in my heart after being prayed for, a new perception burst into my understanding: Jesus desired me! I couldn't believe it. I always knew He loved me. But I assumed that this was a heavenly sort of posture towards all of creation. I never knew that He wanted me, longed for me, and desired me with real emotions.

I had always lived my life with my focus on trying to increase my desire for Him in order to hold on to Him. Now I was overcome with the realization that He desired me more than I had ever desired Him. In fact, He desired me more than I had ever desired anything in my life, including sin! And it was His desire for me that kept me close to Him, not my desire for Him! I tried to express this in song:

Come love of Mine and I will be your home.
Do not wander any longer looking for a heart to own,
for in My heart I carry a hidden sanctuary.
Come love of Mine and I will be your home.

Jesus what a blessed mystery
that Your love should reach through history.
I have wanted to discover
all my life the perfect lover.
And now that I have seen Your face
my search has ended in the place
where Your love
is poured out
with Your life.

Come love of Mine and I will be your home.
Do not wander any longer looking for a heart to own,
for in My heart I carry a hidden sanctuary.
Come love of Mine and I will be your home.

How can I shun such desire?
How could I turn down the honour?
All the time that I spent looking
You were at my door just waiting,
and now that I have heard Your song
I finally know that all along
It was You
who first sang
it to me, singing:

Come love of Mine and I will be your home.
Do not wander any longer looking for a heart to own,
for in My heart I carry a hidden sanctuary.
Come love of Mine and I will be your home.

This intimacy with Christ has catapulted me ahead in my

walk with Him. I have more victory over sin than I have ever had before, because I love Him more than I ever have before. It is much harder to hurt Him or displease him. And being with Him is such a pleasure I am not as tempted to leave that presence. This is entirely to His credit.

A few more things about receiving this blessing. As I have already said, I did not find it easy to receive from the Vineyard. They seemed to have a lot of what I wanted, but they also had a lot of what I did not want. I did not want the culture that seemed to go along with the Vineyard. My perspective was that the Vineyard attracted a lot of hurting, needy people. They seemed to be rather *Californian* in their approach and I found them too casual and laidback. They were very 'low church' whereas I was looking for 'high church'. It was only after I had humbled myself to be ministered to by them that I realized that there was something inevitable about my having to receive Christ from those I did not look up to. Renewal movements often reveal new leaders who are not from the established parts of religious society, and who are often less respected and educated. This was true of Jesus and His disciples. These men were not established, educated leaders whom society respected. The people that swarmed around Jesus and quickly received His Kingdom were not the Pharisees and Sadducees. It was the needy who first responded to Jesus. Paul, the educated one with status, had to be rebuked by the Lord first before he received the Kingdom into his life. I was another who had to receive the rebuke before the blessing.

Because I did not consider myself needy, it was hard for me to receive the new work of God's anointing in my life. This is true of many people. It is probably true of most church leaders today. It is very hard to receive a new work of God because we have to receive it from others who have received it first, and they are usually 'the broken ones'. They were more aware of their need, and so were the first to receive. If we could acknowledge that we are truly needy we might then have the humility to receive more. 'Blessed are those who hunger and thirst for righteousness, for they will be filled.'

I do not feel that God has asked me to abandon my aesthetic sensibilities and resign myself to go culturally slumming for the rest of my life in order to have my spiritual needs met. I *have* had to humble myself and repent of my superiority, and that has been good for me. I look forward to the fruit of disciplined thought and art applied to the work of God's Spirit today. I take consolation in the fact that the renewal under Luther began with bar songs turned into worship songs, which at that time were called chorales. Two hundred years later, J.S. Bach built the greatest masterpieces of western music on just such humble tunes. The exalted expression of worship that I yearn for musically must of necessity have its beginnings in the simple language of a renewal movement.

God bless the ministry of the Vineyard for receiving this blessing from God and passing it on to me.

Richard Riss, *11 August 1994*

Richard is the author of A Survey of 20th-Century Revival Movements in North America, *and is completing his Ph.D. in church history. Over the 'E' mail, he began hearing reports on the meetings at the Airport Vineyard. In June, he went to Rockville Centre, Long Island, and met with the Arnotts who were guest speakers at the Metro Vineyard.*

One of the first indications that what we are now experiencing is a genuine move of the Spirit was the fact that people kept referring to Toronto as the specific geographical location for the outpouring. I saw an immediate parallel with previous revivals, such as the Azusa Street revival, which emanated from Los Angeles, and the Latter Rain revival, which originated in North Battleford, Saskatchewan. In such cases, the way the revival spreads is exactly the same: people go to a specific location from all over the world, then return to bring the revival to their home churches; those who are on the scene of the initial impetus of the revival begin to go to many different places to spread it wherever they go. Note that it is not only a specific city or town that is involved in the origins of a revival, but a specific church (or prayer meeting) within that town. It is almost always in a humble, unexpected place from which these things originate, and there is such a sense of the presence of the Lord that huge numbers of people are drawn from all over the world.

Along with one (or more) fountainhead fellowships or churches, there are usually a few individuals who, themselves, function as springs of revival. For example, in 1948, it was William Branham in North Battleford whom God was using to foment revival, but his only connection with North Battleford was that some people had gone to some of his meetings in Vancouver and brought the anointing back with them to the Sharon Orphanage and Schools in North Battleford. In the same way, Randy Clark and the Arnotts seem to have brought the anointing from Rodney Howard Browne to Toronto.

I have spent several years studying the parallels between the Azusa Street revival (1906) and that in North Battleford (1948), and when I started reading the reports from Toronto, it was immediately clear to me that we had yet another parallel movement going on. It was exactly the same story again. It was quite stunning – like having been away on a voyage, lost, and suddenly finding familiar territory again when you would least have expected it. There's simply no way to describe the thrill of finding something so precious so unexpectedly. To use another analogy, it would be very much like a jeweller finding a rival to the Hope Diamond during the course of normal, everyday activities while working with semi-precious stones. If the jeweller is experienced and well-trained, he recognizes the stone almost immediately. That's how it was for me. I was absolutely stunned, and excited beyond imagining!

God bless all of you!

Mike Turrigiano, *15 June 1994*
(an edited transcription of the Airport Pastors' meeting)

I am the pastor of the Manhattan, New York City Vineyard, and good friends with the Arnotts. I received an urgent call three months ago to come up to Toronto, and my story is much like the other stories you've heard.

The Lord has released something *new* in my life, and in my wife's life, and I'm telling you, I'm talking from the perspective of a person that has had the privilege of experiencing an outpouring back in 1981, '82 and '83, that was written up as the 'third wave'. I was in some of the meetings that John White writes about in his book, *When the Spirit Comes with Power.* To be able to have the privilege of experiencing **twice** in my lifetime what some have only read about in books, and have gone a whole life time praying, 'Lord, come . . .' – I don't have words to express my gratitude to my Father. I don't know why He's been so good.

But I tell you this: I cannot stand here and say, *'Yeah, I've seen it before, nothing new to learn . . . I've had it, seen it, done it, experienced it, back in 1982.'* No, no, no, no, no; there are similarities, but there are some dynamics of this move of the Spirit that are definitely different.

There is the dynamic of coming again, and again, and again, and again, and again, and not getting enough of the presence of the Lord. There's a greater joy, a greater release, a *refreshing* that's happening now, that marks all of this off from the wave of the Spirit in the early '80s.

I think this is undergirded by a fresh revelation of the Father's love; a revelation that God has been impressing on so many of our churches, thanks to men like John Wimber and Ed Piorick who have helped us understand the importance of our relationship with our *Abba*.

Back in the early '80s, God was breaking our pharisaism – you know, we were pharisees, and God had to break that in us. In the early '80s, I was young, radical, headstrong and insecure, and when, by His grace, God met me, and released an impartation of power and authority, I mishandled it. I used it to prove something to others, and to myself; that I AM called, that I AM important. It was a case of *'Listen to me!'*

I was so insecure . . . It was a very hard time, and a season I thought was going to last forever. It felt like there was a mourning that took place inside of me, especially when I thought of the ways I misused the treasure that God had graciously entrusted to me; it was like sand being poured out into my hand, running through it.

As God started to lay a new foundation of healing in my life, I've come to know God as my Father – as Jesus knew Him as Father – and I've learned that the Lord's ministry flowed out of a response to love; it was not a way of gaining recognition, or a way of gaining love. As He stood in the Jordan river, *before* He had performed any miracles, *before* He had peached any sermons, *before* He had raised the dead, *before* He had healed the lepers, *before* He had gone to the cross, His Father broke open heaven and said, 'YOU are my son, in whom I am well pleased.'

I interpret that as, 'Son, there is nothing You can do, there is nothing You have to do for Me to love You; You are the apple of My eye.' And out of *that* affirmation, that mind-blowing affirmation – something most of us have never had – Jesus was able to go forth and face opposition.

There was no fear of man in Him, because He was accepted by the Father; there was no need to manipulate people, nothing He had to do to get people to like Him, because He knew He was loved. The strength, the courage, His ability to stay clean and not get trapped, all had to do with His *identity* built on the foundation of the Father's love.

As we've come to know that, it's been my heart's cry, *'Lord, would you give us another chance?'* I wasted it. I speak for no one else – there were other guys that I've served with, more mature – they didn't waste it, but I did, so I've been saying to the Lord, *'One more chance, one more chance.'*

When John Arnott called, I had two reactions, *'Ah, I don't know . . .'* and what the Holy Spirit spoke to my heart: *'Here's the chance, Mike. Check it out. What have you got to lose?'* I came up to Toronto, and as I've reflected on my experience, I've concluded that this move of God, this outpouring of the Holy Spirit is not separate from coming to know God as our Father. It's not all broken up into different aspects. His wonderful plan for His Church is a continuous flow of life from the Father's heart to the Church.

That foundation of the Father's love is so important for us as pastors because most of us are so insecure. In Acts 6, the beginning of the Church, the infant stages of revival, we read that 'the Word of God spread more and more widely; the number of disciples in Jerusalem was increasing rapidly, and very many of the priests adhered to the faith' (Acts 6:7). My heart's yearning is that we priests, we shepherds, would be healed. Because when we're healed, there's going to be a tremendous release through the Body, and beyond. Maybe we'll move from refreshing to revival.

I'm part of a church that has planted three other churches; I view myself as a catalyst, a 'pyromaniac' – when I was here three months ago, one of the pastors was saying he was a 'pyro', lighting fires for the Lord. I think that's what the Lord has me doing, stirring things up, and it's my desire to see this refreshing outpouring work its way out into the life of the Church so that it produces ministry, so that we look more like Jesus as a Body. As a pastor, with our pastors, we talk about how we do this all the time. Back in New York, in our staff meetings, and dialoguing with the guys up here, we're continually talking about how we move from **raw power** to where it starts to make some sense, so that 'MORE LORD', starts to mean, *'More unto something'*, more unto Christ-likeness, and Kingdom ministry, and relationship with Him. In our meetings, we've begun to pray, 'Lord, birth ministries out of this, inside the church, and out.' That's become our heart's cry. That, because I believe that all this present renewal and impartation is going somewhere. The Lord has a definite direction and destination for all of this.

I think of Ezekiel's vision of the river in chapter 47. In the vision, it starts out as just a trickle, but gradually becomes a powerful river flowing into the Dead Sea, and brings everything to life. This is a picture of God's Spirit bringing refreshment and renewal to the Church, and eventually, revival and life to the lost, the spiritually dead.

In my opinion, this current outpouring of the Holy Spirit is not just for the Church. I believe there's an invitation going out right now. We're being invited to step into the flow of God's Spirit and allow Him to carry us from present renewal, out beyond our meetings and conferences, into life-giving, Spirit-initiated and empowered ministry to the unchurched and lost all around us. I believe that all who get into the Spirit's flow, and who are willing to go deeper, and deeper, and deeper – will end up 'working the nets and cleaning the fish' (see Ezekiel 47:10).

In his *Narrative of Surprising Conversions*, Jonathan Edwards recorded two personal testimonies 'to give a clear idea of the nature and manner of the operation of God's Spirit, in this wonderful effusion of it.' It is hoped that the preceding record accomplishes the same purpose.

Whatever conclusions one draws, they will be as Edwards gave them expression in *Thoughts Concerning the Present Revival of Religion, and the way in which it ought to be acknowledged and promoted:*

> At a time when God manifests Himself in such a great work for His Church, there is no such thing as being neuters; there is a necessity of being either for or against the King that then gloriously appears (I.380a).

CHAPTER SIX

CATCH THE FIRE

Summary and Synthesis

He will baptize you with the Holy Spirit and fire. (Luke 3:16)

There is a story, set in the deserts of Egypt, and at least fifteen hundred years old, that serves as a metaphor, a picture, for the renewing, reviving work of God at the Toronto Airport Vineyard. It takes place between two monks, a junior and a senior; two men who have committed their lives to loving God with all their hearts, and practising hospitality and blessing to any who would come for counsel and spiritual guidance, for prayer, ministry and healing.

> Brother Lot went to see Brother Joseph and said: 'Brother, as much as I am able, I practise a little fasting, some prayer and meditation, and remain quiet, and as much as possible, I keep my thoughts clean. What else should I do?'
>
> The old man stood up and stretched out his hands towards heaven, and his fingers became like ten torches of flame. He said, 'Become *FIRE*!!!'[1]

[1] Yushi Nomura, *Desert Wisdom: Sayings from the Desert Fathers*, Image Books, New York, 1984, p.90.

While not diminishing the importance of the spiritual disciplines in the least, the story is declarative of what has been the experience of thousands of men and women who hunger to answer Christ's call on their lives. As Martyn Lloyd-Jones has stated, 'the Church today needs to be aroused, to be awakened, to be filled with a spirit of glory, for she is failing in the modern world.'[2] With best-intentioned efforts, innumerable pastors and leaders have come under the counsel of growth and business management strategies, and many have run aground, if not exhausted themselves and the churches they serve, in their attempts to bring new life to troubled institutions. Some have bankrupted themselves asking, yet again, 'What else should I do?'

G. Campbell Morgan names the contrast in his reflections on the Welsh revival of 1904-1905:

> If you and I could stand above Wales, looking at it, you would see fire breaking out here and there, and yonder, and somewhere else, without any collusion or pre-arrangement. It is a divine visitation in which God – let me say this reverently – in which God is saying to us, 'See what I can do without the things you are depending on'; 'See what I can do in answer to a praying people'; 'See what I can do through the simplest who are ready to fall in line and depend wholly and absolutely upon Me.'[3]

[2] Martyn Lloyd Jones, *Joy Unspeakable: Power and Renewal in the Holy Spirit*, Shaw Publishers, Wheaton, 1984, p.75.

[3] G. Campbell Morgan, 'The Revival: Its Source and Power', in *Glory Filled the Land: A Trilogy on The Welsh Revival*, ed. Richard Owen Roberts, International Awakening Press, Wheaton, 1989, p.174.

In that spirit of divine encounter, the Scriptural witness to the manifest presence of the Spirit is always marked by bold, declarative and experiential language. On receiving the revelation of the coming of the Lord's glory, the prophet Habakkuk says:

> I hear, and my body quakes;
> my lips quiver at the sound;
> weakness overcomes my limbs,
> and my feet totter in their tracks;
> I long for the day of disaster
> to dawn over our assailants . . .
> I shall exult in the Lord
> and rejoice in the God who saves me.
> The Lord God is my strength;
> He makes me as sure-footed as a hind
> and sets my feet on the heights.
> (Habakkuk 3:3-4, 16, 18-19).

The Apostle Paul pushes the experiential to the forefront when he says: 'To prove that you are sons, God has sent into our hearts the Spirit of His Son, crying, *Abba, Father!* You are therefore no longer a slave but a son, and if a son, an heir by God's own act' (Galatians 4:6-7; see also Romans 8:14-17). The adopting, transforming and energizing power of the Spirit is not religious fluff and splash – it is the very spirituality and mission of the Church of the Risen Christ.

Throughout the history of the Church, the experience of the renewing, reviving work of the Spirit is the very dynamism that breathes vitality and re-formation into what is prone to degenerate into empty ritual and institutionalism. A brief historical summary demonstrates this fact.

In the journals that John Wesley kept there are recorded numerous accounts of the manifestations of the presence and power of the Holy Spirit. A small sample follows.

> At New Year's 1739, George Whitefield, my brother Charles, three others and I, with about sixty of our brethren, were present at a love feast in Fetter Lane. About three in the morning, as we were continuing in prayer, the power of God came upon us so mightily that many cried out in holy joy, while others were knocked to the ground. As soon as we were recovered a little from awe and amazement at the presence of God, we broke out in one voice, 'We praise Thee, O God; we acknowledge Thee to be the Lord.'[4]
>
> Thursday, preaching at Newgate . . . one, then another, and another sunk to the earth; they dropped on every side as if thunderstruck. One of them cried aloud. We besought God on her behalf and He turned her heaviness into joy. A second being in the same agony, we called upon God for her also; He spoke peace unto her soul.[5]
>
> Friday evening I went to a society at Wapping, weary in body and faint in spirit . . . . After I had finished preaching and was earnestly inviting all sinners

[4] *John Wesley's Journal*, vol. II, ed. N. Curnock. London, p.122.
[5] *Ibid.*, II.182.

to enter into the holiest by this new and living way, many of those who had heard began to call upon God with strong cries and tears. Some sank down, having no strength remaining in them. Others trembled and quaked exceedingly. Some were torn with a kind of convulsive motion in every part of their bodies, often so violently that sometimes four or five persons could not hold one of them. I have seen many hysterical and many epileptic fits, but in most respects none of them were like these. I immediately prayed that God would not allow those who were weak to be offended.[6]

A less well-known figure named Daniel Rowland served as one of the revival preachers in Wales. Letters written to his friend George Whitefield record some of the unforgettable scenes witnessed:

While one is praying, another is laughing; some howl and beat their hands together; others are weeping and groaning; and others are grovelling on the ground in a swoon, making various kinds of antic postures; then they laugh out all at once, and continue laughing for about a quarter of an hour.[7]

The power that continues with [Brother Rowland] is uncommon. Such crying out and heart-breaking groans, silent weeping and holy joy and shouts of rejoicing, I never saw. 'Tis very common when he

[6] *Ibid.*, II.221.

[7] *Daniel Rowland and the Great Evangelical Awakening in Wales.* Eifon Evans, Banner of Truth Trust, Edinburgh, 1985, p.158.

> preaches for scores to fall down by the power of the Word, pierced and wounded or overcome by the love of God, and sights of the beauty and excellency of Jesus . . . Some lie [on the floor] for hours, some praising and admiring Jesus; others wanting for words to utter. You might read the language of a heart running over with love in their heavenly looks, their eyes sparkling with the fire of love and joy and solid rest in God.[8]

On another occasion, the bi-polar reactions to the Spirit's ministry in Rowland's preaching were described as follows:

> Some souls in this meeting were feasting at their heavenly Father's table. Some were drunk, and that with the best wine, namely, the Holy Spirit, God's peace, God's love shed abroad in their hearts by the Holy Ghost. Some prominent people scorn and deride this, but it is the substance of religion.[9]

This love/hate response to the dynamics of renewal and revival is a characteristic response to the outpouring of God's Spirit down through the ages, and is easily traced at the Airport Vineyard meetings. In an article published in the *Christian Research Newsletter*, the 'holy laughter at the Ontario Vineyard' is more than cautiously described.

> . . . Pastor John Arnott [made] reference to themes

[8] *Ibid.*, p.217.
[9] *Ibid.*, p.380.

> [that] conservative evangelicals would consider soundly biblical – assurance of the Father's love, Christian unity, loving service, the needs for worldwide revival in the Church, deliverance from bitterness and unforgiving attitudes, and a call to repent of sin and accept Christ.
>
> However, the service seemed to be overshadowed by activity of questionable biblical meaning or purpose. Arm- and head-shaking, foot-stamping, chair-rocking, and above all laughter; loud, at times almost hysterical, wails from some individuals frequently permeated the large auditorium . . .

The evaluations of Dr Daniel Lundy, president of the Toronto Baptist Seminary and pastor of Jarvis Street Baptist Church, are featured at the end of the article:

> 'When the Vineyard raises hopes for dramatic supernatural intervention, Dr Lundy says he and his fellow pastors have to deal with their shattered expectations.'[10]

Those who have been the *subjects* of 'dramatic supernatural intervention' at the meetings at the Airport Vineyard echo and re-echo the testimony recorded under Rowland's ministry in the Welsh revival:

> There fell upon us the sweet breath of the love of the Lord. The fire was kindled . . . Gone was unbelief,

[10] *Christian Research Newsletter*, volume 2, issue 2, P.O. Box 3216, Station B, Calgary, Alberta, April/May 1994, pp.3-4.

> gone guilt, gone fear, gone a timid, cowardly spirit, lack of love, envy, suspicion . . . and in their place came love, faith, hope, a joyful spirit, with a glorious multitude of the graces of the Holy Spirit.[11]

Even with such declarative witness to liberating gospel dynamics, the question is always being asked: 'Is this a genuine work of God?' Back in 1762, the following assessment was given, and it more than serves as the question is brought forward in our day:

> It is not only by means of outward manifestations, such as shouting, jumping, laughing, that I conclude that God is in the Church and is visiting His people. Apart from the heavenly inclination on their spirits inciting their tongues to a lively praising of God, this fire burns in the life and behaviour of so many of them . . . . They are zealous, not for secondary matters of faith, but for the essential issues of salvation. Faith and love are the chief graces they cry for . . .[12]

Those that give their testimony at the Airport Vineyard come from all walks of life. Some struggle for words that adequately describe what they have experienced; some are gifted with an eloquence that enables them to give almost poetic expression to the work of the Spirit. Such was the case with Henry Alline, a preacher of the

[11] Eifon Evans, *Op. cit.*, p.314.
[12] *Ibid.*, p.321.

Awakening, who served in Nova Scotia and the Eastern Seaboard. From his journal, we read of the Spirit's renewing, reviving work two hundred and ten years ago:

> O the sweetness of release, when the mourning soul has long been bowed down under doubts and fears, temptations and trails; and when the blessed Redeemer, who is their soul's chief delight, stirs up His Kingdom in their hearts, gives them the communication of divine grace, and comforts their drooping spirits with the smiles of Heaven. O the happy exchange from chains to liberty; from darkness to light; from grief to joy; from mourning to rejoicing; from captivity to victory: then they can lean on the breast of their Beloved, and rejoice in His glorious name. O there is none that can tell the sweetness of His love, but those that have enjoyed it.'[13]

The reviving work of the Spirit is not confined to the eighteenth century. The year 1801 marks the zenith of what is known as 'The Second Great Awakening'. The geographical centre for this remarkable move of God was Cane Ridge, Kentucky. The crowds that assembled for the protracted meetings numbered between ten and twenty thousand, and people came from as far away as Ohio and Tennessee. To put some perspective on the size of the crowd, Lexington, Kentucky's largest town at the

[13] *The Journal of Henry Alline*, eds. James Beverly and Barry Moody, Lancelot Press, Hantsport, Nova Scotia, 1982, p.123.

time, had a population of 1,800.[14] One of the leading evangelists was a frontiersman named Peter Cartwright, a circuit rider with the Methodist Episcopal Church. He had calculated that he preached at least 14,600 sermons, received into the Church at least 10,000 adult members, and baptized almost the same number of children.[15] In his *Autobiography,* Cartwright comments on the 'mighty power of God' that was witnessed at the camp meetings: the following are his reflections on one of the phenomenon witnessed.

> In the midst of our controversies on the subject of the powerful exercises among the people under preaching, a new exercise broke out among us, called the *jerks,* which was overwhelming in its effects upon the bodies and minds of the people. No matter whether they were saints or sinners, they would be taken under a warm song or sermon, and seized with a convulsive jerking all over, which they could not by any possibility avoid, and the more they resisted the more they jerked. If they would not strive against it and pray in good earnest, the jerking would usually abate. I have seen more than five hundred persons jerking at one time in my large congregations. Most usually persons taken with the jerks, to obtain relief, as they said, would rise up and dance. Some would run, but could not get away. Some would resist; on such the jerks were generally very severe.

[14] Keith Hardman, *The Spiritual Awakeners,* Moody Bible Institute, Chicago, 1983, p. 137.
[15] *Ibid.*, p.146.

> To see those proud young gentlemen and young ladies, dressed in their silks, jewelry, and prunella, from top to toe, take the *jerks,* would often [cause *me* to laugh!] The first jerk or so, you would see their fine bonnets, caps, and combs fly; and so sudden would be the jerking of the head that their long loose hair would crack almost as loud as a wagoner's whip.

The 'jerks' is one of the manifestations witnessed at the Airport meetings, and it IS very funny to watch one so affected! By times, it is as if someone hits the 'afflicted' with a cattle prod, so violent is the response. It is, however, not the outward reaction, but the inner transformation that is of consequence. Though suffering erratic convulsions, one man was so grateful for the newness of life he experienced in Christ, that he proudly wore a T-shirt he had printed: 'I'm a JERK FOR JESUS!'

Peter Cartwright not only documents the manifestation; he records his reflection and evaluation of the phenomenon:

> I always looked upon the jerks as a judgement sent from God, first, to bring sinners to repentance; and, secondly, to show professors that God could work with or without means, and that He could work over and above means, and do whatsoever seemed [to] Him good, to the glory of His grace and the salvation of the world.[16]

[16] *The Autobiography of Peter Cartwright,* Abingdon, Nashville, 1956, pp. 45-46.

He notes that many 'weak-minded, ignorant and superstitious persons' fake the jerks, so as to draw attention to themselves; nevertheless, 'with many, it was involuntary'. Cartwright's practice was to recommend to those jerking the practice of fervent prayer as remedy. 'It almost universally proved an effective antidote.'[17]

Revival leaders down through the ages have continuously stressed that the physical and emotional manifestations of the Spirit's presence must never be the index of spiritual power or even reality. William Blair comments on the particular phenomenon of 'prostration, what is commonly called *striking down*'. He forthrightly titles his treatise, *Things Which Have Been Seen And Heard;* the revival he is documenting took place in Northern Ireland, August 1859. He states:

> Too little as well as too much has been made of the singular physical features of this great revival. By some they are regarded as [abnormal and excessive]. I do not think so. They have accompanied all revivals . . . I care not what sceptics may say, or little-faith Christians, who have no confidence in the extraordinary influences of the Spirit. I believe, as firmly as I believe my own existence, that the Holy Ghost would never have permitted His work to be entangled with such perplexing and seemingly incredible phenomena, had He not had a most important end to serve by them.[18]

[17] *Ibid.*

[18] *Authentic Records of Revival,* ed. William Reid, James Nisbet, London, 1860, pp.47 and 49.

Blair concludes his work with three testimonies, one of which is the report of a man who 'was overcome and lay quiet for six hours, and then got peace'. He had stuttered from birth, and was 'miraculously restored to speech', a healing certified by a local notary. He was also delivered from his 'inordinate addiction' to tobacco and spirits.[19]

In 1892 an outburst of criticism brought indictment against Ralph Horner, an ex-Methodist evangelist who travelled the Ottawa Valley of Ontario and Quebec. He was accused of 'preaching prostration', because so many came under the power of the Spirit when he ministered. Like Wesley before him, Horner believed that while it was not appropriate to call people to fall down, neither did he condemn it. He never encouraged physical manifestations or contended for them; as it is recorded in the *Memoirs* compiled by his wife, 'he maintained that under the mighty outpouring of the Holy Spirit such scenes would follow.'[20]

Revival phenomena have been well documented in outpourings of the Spirit in more recent history. Richard Riss' *Survey of Twentieth Century Revival Movements in North America* serves as a helpful description and assessment of the early Pentecostal outpouring, the 'latter rain' movement of the 1940s and '50s, the Jesus People and the charismatic renewal.

[19] *Ibid.*, p.58.

[20] A. E. Horner, *Ralph C. Horner, Evangelist,* Henderson Printing, Inc., Brockville Ontario, 1994, p.xiii.

Students of revival will have been familiar with many of the leaders mentioned in this summary, and they will have their own favourite stories to re-tell. The history of revival dynamisms, however, is not confined to the last two hundred and fifty years. Howard Snyder helpfully traces God's renewing work, focusing on four movements that illuminate what he describes as the *reshaping* of the Church: Montanism, the Church's 'first charismatic movement'; German Pietism under Johann Arndt's leadership; Moravianism, Count Zinzendorf and the Herrnhut community; and Methodism and the cell-based structure initiated by John Wesley.[21]

Snyder's study can easily be complemented, for throughout the history of the early centuries of the Church, there are eloquent witnesses to the renewing, reviving work of the Spirit of God. Hilary of Poitiers, a theologian whose writings influenced Augustine and Ambrose, wrote a work titled, *On the Trinity* (356-359), and another, a *Tract on the Psalms* (364-367). In both, he writes about baptism and the impartation of the Holy Spirit in the believer's life. Hilary comments on Jesus' invitation in John 7:37-39, 'If anyone is thirsty, let him come to Me and drink. Whoever believes in Me, as Scripture says, "Streams of living water shall flow from within him".'

> The Holy Spirit is called a river. When we receive the Holy Spirit, we are made drunk. Because out of us, as

[21] Howard Snyder, *Signs of the Spirit*, Zondervan, Grand Rapids, 1989.

> a source, various streams of grace flow, the prophet prays that the Lord will inebriate us. The prophet wants the same persons to be made drunk, and filled to all fullness with the divine gifts, so that their generation may be multiplied. This means that the good earth is compared in the gospel simile to the seed of the word, bearing fruit thirty, sixty and a hundred fold.
>
> We who have been reborn through the sacrament of baptism experience intense joy when we feel within us the first stirrings of the Holy Spirit. We begin to have insight into the mysteries of faith, we are able to prophesy and to speak with wisdom. We become steadfast in hope and receive the gifts [plural] of healing. Demons are made subject to our authority.
>
> These gifts enter us like a gentle rain, and once having done so, little by little, bring forth fruit in abundance. When this gentle rain falls, the earth rejoices. The rains are multiplied so that, at first, there are small streams; the streams then become raging rivers, so that they become mighty rivers.[22]

Hilary makes at least two points explicitly: one, that God is exceedingly generous in pouring out His Spirit; and two, that the *end* and *purpose* of the outpouring is mission and ministry.

Roughly ten years later, another of the Church

[22] Hilary of Poitiers, *Tract on the Psalms,* 64.6ff; see Kilan McDonnell and George Montague, *Christian Initiation and Baptism in the Holy Spirit,* Liturgical Press, Collegeville, Minnesota, 1991, pp. 144-55.

Fathers, Basil the Great, Archbishop of Caeserea, authored a treatise titled *On the Holy Spirit*. He wrote the work because of a movement known as the Arian heresy. Central to the theological distortion that Arius imposed was the lowering of the dignity of both Jesus and the Holy Spirit: speaking of the Trinity, Arius maintained, 'There is a triad, not in equal glories.'[23]

In his defence of the Spirit, Basil writes of the present-day ministry of the Paraclete, the Revealer (John 14:26; 16:7-15). On the forefront of the Spirit's work is a renewing, reviving dynamism that produces mission, and growth in holiness.

> Just as when a sunbeam falls on bright and transparent bodies, they themselves become brilliant too, and shed forth a fresh brightness from themselves, so souls wherein the Spirit dwells, illuminated by the Spirit, themselves become spiritual, and send forth their grace to others.
>
> [From the Spirit] comes foreknowledge of the future, understanding of mysteries, apprehension of what is hidden, the distribution of wonderful charisms (gifts), a citizenship in heaven, *a dance with angels* and *joy without end,* resting in God, and highest of all, [Christlikeness].[24]

[23] *Nicene and Post-Nicene Fathers, Second Series,* vol. VIII, Hendrickson Publications, Peabody, 1994, p.1.
[24] *Ibid.*, pp.15-16.

Even if one should literally 'dance with Angels', such ecstasy is secondary. Though it has been sounded again and again, it needs to be reiterated: while an outpouring of the manifest presence of the Spirit of God often generates unusual religious experience and phenomena, the focus must never be on the shaking, falling, wailing or roaring, as commanding as these manifestations may be. They are but signals, or pointers, to a much larger dynamism.

A simple illustration is helpful. Most of us have a driver's licence; many of us own a car. Very few of us have either just so that we can sit in the driver's seat and operate the turn indicators. We have our licence, and own our vehicles, in order to get somewhere; signalling the journey lets others know where we're headed, and as such, is helpful, but relatively incidental. Some, in fact, travel without signalling; they arrive at their destination nonetheless.

From the first chapter of this book, recall Annie Dillard's reflections on worship – that in offering ourselves to the Lord, God indeed chooses to 'draw us out to where we can never return'. This has been the case for countless thousands who have received the Lord's outpouring of grace upon grace. The visitation of the Spirit at the Toronto Airport Vineyard has forced many of us to reshuffle pre-suppositions and expectations; it has knocked out the ends of the box in which we had neatly contained our God. We have re-oriented ourselves, and are beginning to understand the truth that Eduard Schweizer declares: 'Long before the Spirit was a theme of doctrine, He was a *fact* in the experience of the [early Church].'[25] A spirit of repentance has risen up, for with new eyes to see, we realize that we have boxed God in quite tidily; many of us have lived, operatively, believing in 'Father, Son, and Holy Book'; and we confess to having trifled with the charge of being Christ's ambassadors.

Many of us have now touched, as never before, something of our Lord's resurrection power and presence, the very realities of the Gospel. We know more of holy fear and holy joy. Much is still a mystery; but with the unanswered questions, there has risen up a healthy humility and openness to receive what the Sovereign Lord has for His Church. As this move of God continues to gain momentum, as hundreds gather night after night, and as pastors and leaders return to their churches all around the world, this renewing, reviving work of God has been, for thousands, an *awakening.*

Joseph Hazzaya and his writings serve by way of conclusion. Hazzaya is one of the great Syrian theologians, wedding together what is so frequently kept poles apart – dynamic spiritual experience, and speculative understanding. As a monk, he was known as 'Abdisho', 'The Seer'. The details of his life are unclear; he lived through the turn of the eighth century. In his

[25] Eduard Schweizer, 'Pneuma', *Theological Dictionary of the New Testament,* Eerdmans, Grand Rapids, 1968, vol. VI, p.396.

Book of Questions, he addresses the same issues that caused me to write this book: *How the Spirit which works in us is known, in what His power is revealed, and what is the sign by which the Spirit makes manifest His working in us.* Hazzaya writes nearly 1300 years ago, and uses beautiful, though somewhat unfamiliar language and phraseology to describe the impartation of the Spirit that the believer receives at baptism. With wise counsel undiminished over time, he marks four signals of the Spirit's powerful presence:

> The first sign of the effective working of the Spirit is when the love of God burns in the heart of a man like fire . . .
>
> The second sign through which you will feel that the Spirit which you received from baptism is working in you, consists in true humility being born in your soul . . . It is from humility that peace, meekness and endurance of tribulations are born in the soul.
>
> The third sign of the working of the Spirit in you consists in the [compassion] which represents within you the image of God, through which, when your thoughts extend to all men, tears flow from your eyes like fountains of water, as if all men were dwelling in your heart, and you affectionately embrace them and kiss them, while you pour your kindness on all. When you remember them, your heart is kindled with the power of the working of the Spirit in you as with fire, and from this, goodness and kindness are born in your heart.

> The fourth sign of the working of the Spirit which you received in baptism consists in the illumined vision of your mind . . . It is this vision that receives the light of the Holy Trinity. From this . . . you will derive a flow of spiritual speech and the knowledge of both worlds: of the one that has passed and the one that shall pass, and also a consciousness of the mysteries of future things, the fine sounds of the spiritual intelligences: joy, jubilation, exultation, glorification, songs, hymns, and odes of magnification.
>
> The above are the signs, which if you find in yourself, you will know that the Holy Spirit, which you received from the holy baptism, is working in you.[26]

If we move from a consideration of water baptism, to the prophetic announcement of John the Baptist, that the coming Messiah 'will baptize with the Holy Spirit and with fire', all of this takes on even greater consequence. The phrase, 'He will baptize' is a technical one, taken from the wool market. Raw wool was plunged into a vat of dye, stirred around and around until the whole thing was saturated in the colour of the dye. The greek word to describe this process comes from the root *baptidzo*, 'to baptize'.

The prophet presents us with a graphic picture. 'He

[26] Alphonse Mirgana, *Early Christian Mystics,* Cambridge, Heffer and Sons, 1934, pp. 165–67.

will baptize you . . . *with the Holy Spirit and with fire.'* As we are baptized in the Spirit, and the fire of God, we are, as it were, plunged, stirred about, and saturated. It may be that some of the unusual physical manifestations witnessed at the Airport Vineyard can be understood as the Lord *saturating* His people with the Holy Spirit and with fire.

Many of us who have come to the meetings recognize that we're 'tie-dyed' believers.

Tie-dying was a fashion vogue twenty years ago; T-shirts were tied in knots, and then 'baptized' into various pots of dye. When dry, they were untied, and patterns resulted showing differentiated colour penetration.

Each of us have areas of our lives that are knotted up; some of us have whole sections of our lives closed off such that they don't get all fired up, and drenched in the Holy Spirit. Consequently, those bits don't carry the 'colour' they're supposed to.

The Gospel of Jesus Christ declares that God's Spirit is forever untangling us, untying our knots, letting us loose, and 'saturating' our very being, so that we become more and more like Christ.

If we are to *Catch the Fire*, it is to each of us to say 'Yes Lord,' and let the Spirit release what needs releasing, and fill what needs filling.

By God's grace, may we indeed live out our baptism in *Spirit and fire.*

S.D.G

SELECTED BIBLIOGRAPHY

Angoff, Charles, ed., *Jonathan Edwards: His Life and Influence*, London: Associated University Press, 1975.

Burns, James, *Revivals: Their Laws and Leaders*, London: Hodder and Stoughton, 1909.

Bushman, Richard, ed., *The Great Awakening: Documents on the Revival of Religion, 1740-1745*, New York: Atheneum, 1970.

Cartwright, Peter, *Autobiography*, Nashville: Abingdon, 1956.

Cherry, Conrad, *The Theology of Jonathan Edwards*, Indiana University Press, 1984.

Conken, Paul, *Cane Ridge: America's Pentecost*, University of Wisconsin, 1990.

Drummond, Lewis, *Eight Keys to Biblical Revival*, Minneapolis: Bethany House, 1994.

Dunn, James G. D., *Jesus and the Spirit*, London: SCM Press, 1975.

Edwards, Jonathan, *The Works of Jonathan Edwards*, Edinburgh: The Banner of Truth Trust, 1992.

Evans, Eifon, *Daniel Rowland and the Great Evangelical*

Awakening in Wales, Edinburgh: The Banner of Truth Trust, 1985.

Finney, Charles, *Lectures on Revival,* Minneapolis: Bethany House, 1988.

Hardman, Keith, *The Spiritual Awakeners,* Chicago: Moody Press, 1983.

Heimert, Alan and Miller, Perry, eds., *The Great Awakening: Documents Illustrating the Crisis and Its Consequences,* New York: Bobbs-Merrill Co., 1967.

Hopwood, R. G. S., *The Religious Experience of the Primitive Church,* New York: Scribners' Sons, 1937.

Kerr, Hugh and Mulder, John, eds., *Conversions,* Grand Rapids: Eerdmans, 1983.

Lloyd-Jones, Martyn, *Revival,* Westchester, Illinois: Crossway Books, 1987.

Murray, Iain, *Jonathan Edwards: A New Biography,* Edinburgh: The Banner of Truth Trust, 1992.

McDonnell, Kilian and Montague, George, *Christian Initiation and Baptism in the Holy Spirit,* Collegeville, Minnesota: The Liturgical Press, 1991.

MacNutt, Francis, *Overcome By the Spirit,* Grand Rapids: Chosen Books, 1990, and London: Eagle, 1991.

Pratney, Winkie, *Revival: Its Principles and Personalities,* Lafayette, Louisiana: Huntington House Publishers, 1994.

Riss, Richard, *A Survey of 20th-Century Revival Movements in North America,* Peabody, Massachusetts: Hendrickson, 1988.

Roberts, Richard Owen, ed., *Glory Filled the Land: A Trilogy on the Welsh Revival,* Wheaton: International Awakening Press, 1989.

Simonson, Harold, *Jonathan Edwards: Theologian of the Heart,* Macon, Georgia: Mercer University Press, 1974.

Snyder, Howard, *Signs of the Spirit,* Grand Rapids, Zondervan, 1989.

Terrain, Samuel, *The Elusive Presence,* San Francisco: Harper and Row, 1978.

Tracy, Joseph, *The Great Awakening: A History of The Revival of Religion in the Times of Edwards and Whitefield,* Boston: Charles Tappan, 1845.

Tracy, Patricia, *Jonathan Edwards, Pastor,* New York: Hill and Wang, 1979.

Weakley, Clare, ed., *John Wesley: The Nature of Revival,* Minneapolis: Bethany House, 1987.

White, John, *When the Spirit Comes With Power,* Downers Grove: IVP Press, 1988, and London: Hodder & Stoughton, 1992.